Better Birthing
with Hypnosis

Better Birthing with Hypnosis

Mindful Pregnancy and Easy Labor
Using the Leclaire Childbirth Method

MICHELLE LECLAIRE O'NEILL, PH.D., R.N.

Keats Publishing

Chicago   New York   San Francisco   Lisbon   London   Madrid   Mexico City
Milan   New Delhi   San Juan   Seoul   Singapore   Sydney   Toronto

Library of Congress Cataloging-in-Publication Data

O'Neill, Michelle Leclaire.
   Better birthing with hypnosis : mindful pregnancy and easy labor using the
Leclaire childbirth method / Michelle Leclaire O'Neill.
     p. cm.
   Includes bibliographical references and index.
   ISBN 0-658-01533-8 (alk. paper)
   1. Natural childbirth.   2. Hypnotism in obstetrics.   3. Autogenic training.

  RG661.O569 2001
  618.4'5—dc21

                         2001038351

Keats Publishing

A Division of The McGraw·Hill Companies

1 2 3 4 5 6 7 8 9 10   DOC/DOC   10 9 8 7 6 5 4 3 2 1

ISBN 0-658-01533-8

This book was designed and set in Melior by Laurie Young
Printed and bound by R. R. Donnelley—Crawfordsville

Cover design by Laurie Young
Cover photo © Tony Stone Images

Grateful acknowledgment is made to Jack Crimmins for the use of his poem. Used by permission.

Some parts of this book have appeared in slightly different form in *Creative Childbirth* by Michelle Leclaire O'Neill, Ph.D., R.N.

This book is not intended to replace medical guidance. Persons should consult their physicians or other medical practitioners before following any specific procedure discussed in this book. Responsibility for any adverse effects resulting from the use of information in this book rests solely with the reader.

This book is printed on acid-free paper.

Dedicated to Anne Campion Stewart, R.N., former supervisor of Ob/Gyn at St. Vincent's Hospital in New York City, who had the intuition to change the way newborns were handled throughout the United States and removed from the mothers and isolated in a nursery. It was she who created rooming in so that mother and infant could maintain the bond established in utero and so that baby could feel safe and secure and be cared for by mother. "Twas a little bit of heaven came from out the sky one day," and now you've returned alas not to your Ireland but, I hope, to that little bit of heaven you brought to all who knew you. With the grandest of memories, this book celebrates you.

Also dedicated to Elizabeth Bing, cofounder of the Lamaze Method and continuing mentor to all of us who want to carry on and move into the twenty-first century with the newest scientific information on pregnancy and birth. Thank you for all your work and for paving the way. Thanks to you, each of us is an individual woman giving birth, not just another primip and multip in the "delivery" room.

A feeling of fullness comes,
but usually it takes some bread to bring it.

—RUMI

Contents

Acknowledgments

Much appreciation to Georgia Hughes for her collaboration on this project. I have truly enjoyed and felt supported by our many phone discussions and consultations, and I look forward to our next and newest project together. It is always a delight to work with you. Thank you.

Thanks to Barbara Fuller for her excellent editorial skills. Your organizational ability—knowing exactly what chapter to move, or what phrase or paragraph—and your concise, well-pointed questions were a blessing.

Thanks to Rena Copperman for coming in at the very end and graciously suggesting the necessary finishing touches and reorganization that made a great difference. She made the whole project feel like fun and teamwork.

To Cassidy, my partner, thanks for dealing with all the papers and books, not always contained in the studio. Thanks for your continued love, support, and encouragement and for graciously allowing me the space and time I've needed to write.

To all the amazing mothers and partners with whom I have had the pleasure of working, I thank you for the privilege of participating in your pregnancies, labors, and births, and to all the uborns to whom I have spoken. It continues to be an incredible and awesome experience.

Introduction

Every child deserves a warm welcome into the world, both emotionally and physically. The Leclaire Method of pregnancy and childbirth outlined in this book can help you to achieve such a miraculous beginning for you, your baby, and your family. The focus of this approach is on the connections of mind, body, and spirit, leading to a healthy and conscious pregnancy and a healthy, happy baby. The more intact you feel emotionally and spiritually, the easier it is for your body to adapt to pregnancy, the intensity of labor, and the demands of motherhood. The methods outlined in this book can realistically prepare you for an easy childbirth by providing you with the skills and tools to examine and explore your feelings and, when necessary, to alter your emotions. You will learn a systematic approach using mind and body techniques for managing your pregnancy and labor, and you will learn to communicate with your *uborn* (uterine born) to begin bonding and to enhance mental development prior to birth.

The Leclaire Method is the first childbirth method to be developed by a woman and mother and to focus back on a woman's instinctive ability to birth a child. It is a complete and holistic program that will help you approach pregnancy as the glorious event it should be for both mother and baby. Drawing on both modern science and the ancient wisdom of giving birth, it is a model of natural childbirth that can stand the test of scientific scrutiny because of a single fact: It works!

Your baby's emotional balance depends on her surrounding sensory input. My program will help you to create a healthy, interactive relationship with your uborn and with the person your uborn will become. The purpose of this book is to help you to optimize the prenatal development of your uborn and to help you and your partner to be compassionate with your own needs, desires, and limitations; and to pave the way for a healthy pregnancy, an easy labor and birth, and a healthy, gentle postpartum. These are the precursors to a healthy, happy, joyous, and fulfilling life.

Throughout this book, you will learn aspects of pre- and postnatal care and gain a new understanding of all the influences on the uborn. There is a connection between our thoughts and beliefs and their physical manifestations. Expectant mothers can enhance nourishing experiences and reduce unhealthy influences that affect mother, child, and the family during pregnancy. The brain is very responsive to change and continuously updates its model of reality.

The brain of your baby begins to form in utero and is completed by synaptic connections. These connections are where one nerve cell signals to another. They allow your brain to give and receive messages and can have a profound effect on your emotional, physical, and mental states, even though scientists are not always sure why and how this works. The synaptic connections are different in each individual, and they are dependent on the environment. This book is about creating a wondrous environment for your uborn. Through your actions and through the continuity and stability of your emotional presence, your baby will be able to give rise to not only a healthy body but also a healthy "self."

THE LECLAIRE METHOD

The approach outlined in this book will ease your fear of childbirth and teach you simple ways to reduce pain and to have an easier labor and birth. Along with helping you to develop a positive mother–infant bond, these techniques can prevent low (unhealthy) birth weight, increase your child's innate emotional and intellectual balance, ease the transition to breastfeeding, and create the healthiest possible environment for a new life. Some recent studies have indicated that proper mother–child bonding can prevent attention deficit hyperactivity disorder (ADHD), prevent feelings of abandonment, and create a platform for intelligence and moral behavior. The suggestions in this book can help you to create a climate in which healthy mother–father–infant communications can occur, an environment in which the spirit of your baby will have room to move in you. The new paradigm of pregnancy can be the evolution of the world.

One of the workshops I teach is a one-day, all-day pregnancy retreat called Smart Beginnings. During the course of this class, the mother and her support person use all of the techniques that you'll learn in this book. The day mimics labor in that the support person is there 100 percent. We go through early labor and transition and employ all the techniques for these stages. Mothers and fathers then realize that labor is just an extension of the Smart Beginnings class, just as you will realize that labor is an extension of the techniques you will learn in this book.

As you read through the following chapters, you will learn about the development of the new life in your womb and how you—mother and father—can influence this development for the health, intelligence, and happiness of the baby. The exercises described will enhance the communication of your love and natural happiness for the baby. The Leclaire Method teaches you how to enhance your relationship with your unborn child so that the genetic potential of the uborn can become a reality. The positive and healthy relationship between a pregnant mother and her unborn child gives the infant permission to realize all the wonderful attributes of the individual he will become.

The Leclaire Method explores pregnancy, labor, birthing, and mothering from the following perspectives:

- How interpersonal relationships and beliefs can affect the mother
- How the uborn develops physically and what the physical realities of labor are
- How beliefs can be acknowledged and altered to enhance your experience of pregnancy, labor, and birthing
- How you can use hypnosis and self-hypnosis to calm yourself and remain in control while altering your perception of pain
- How you can change your unhealthy beliefs with rational, thoughtful exercises, meditation, and imagery to overcome the negative effects of emotions such as fear, anger, sadness, and anxiety
- How dreams, both unconscious and conscious, can help mothers and fathers explore their inner lives
- How the gentle use of touch and massage, through hypnotouch, can help mother and baby
- How music and sound can influence mother and child
- How mothers can work with their beliefs toward a more satisfactory experience

By mastering and feeling in control of your pregnancy, you will create stability for your own experience as well as for that of the baby. Every mother should have adequate psychological and social support during her pregnancy. Your relaxation and emotional contentment can bring a peaceful baby into the world. A good pregnancy and birth experience contribute to the health of the baby while they comfort and empower both mother and father. The bonding that is part of my approach creates a supportive environment for the future. With newfound ease, you will create an environment in which the spirit of your baby has room to move in you, to grow into full potential.

We now know that happiness, health, and emotional security begin in utero. Mother–infant bonding and the prevention of child abuse also begin during pregnancy. Throughout your pregnancy, you can transform your experience to create healthy babies, minds, families, and societies. From conception on, your baby is responsive to your ways of being. Your thoughts convey information to the cells of your baby. Your emotions, a result of your thinking, are the link between your mind/body and your baby. You will develop a new admiration of your biochemistry and a deep appreciation of the powers of your mind/body to create a healthy environment for yourself and your baby. This new respect can empower you to desire a conscious pregnancy, allowing for a healthy flow of prenatal communication.

Case Study: Kristina

As a simple example of how a mother–fetal mind/body interaction could affect the life of a newborn, let's look at Baby Kristina. When Kristina was put to her mother's breast soon after birth, she refused to suckle; in subsequent attempts, she continued to refuse her mother's breast. Kristina's pediatrician, a Swede working in a European tradition, asked her mother for permission to try an experiment.[1] All necessary parties agreed, and Kristina was placed at the breast of a mother in an adjacent room. Kristina nursed contentedly. The pediatrician then asked Kristina's mother if she had wanted a baby. She replied that actually she hadn't wanted a baby and

---

1. This study was reported in *The Secret Life of the Unborn Child* by Thomas Verny with Kelly John (New York: Dell Publishing, 1981).

that she had wanted to abort Kristina, but her husband had talked her out of it. It appears that Kristina experienced her mother's original desire and was responding to it after birth by rejecting her breast. Once Kristina's mother understood the cause of Kristina's rejection, she was able to demonstrate love and caring to her new baby, and soon Kristina nursed happily at her mother's breast.

Leclaire can help you take just such negative emotions—or any form of anxiety—and transform them into a healthy approach to your baby and his or her birth. The following chapters will show you how to use this subtle yet powerful communication to nurture your uborn.

ONE BABY AT A TIME

There are many ways to care for yourself and your new baby during pregnancy and postpartum. Techniques of mind/body health, including self-hypnosis, meditation, and visualization or imagery, can help you through all stages of pregnancy as you bond with your infant and prepare yourself and the cherished new life within for birth and for childhood. Your mind is the most powerful tool that you have to promote a healthy pregnancy, a healthy birth, a healthy baby, and an authentic child.

Nutrition and physical health are certainly crucial to a healthy baby, but you should not neglect the emotional, intellectual, and spiritual aspects of nurturing as well. Every mother should have adequate psychological and social support during her pregnancy. Society does not always recognize this need for nurture for women. Your relaxation and emotional contentment can bring a peaceful baby into the world.

PLANNING FOR AN EASY PREGNANCY

As with any new endeavor, the more work you do before you undertake a task, the better prepared you are to perform it. Pregnancy, labor, and birth are natural to women's bodies, but even so, planning ahead will help you be prepared and make the process a familiar one, not something to dread. With that in mind, take some time during the next couple of weeks or at some time during your pregnancy to follow these steps:

1. Read this entire book. Then go back and work through one chapter a week, including the exercises. If you haven't started early, start anyway. Even if you are at week 39, it is better to start now than not to do this at all. OR

2. Take a pregnancy "retreat" day or weekend and do all of the exercises in this book during the retreat. Simply set aside one day or one weekend to do this, whether you go away or stay in your own home.

3. Form your own support group. Gather mothers from your area and meet once a week. Start with listening to the *Hypnosis and Pregnancy* tape (to order tapes, see Resources in the back of this book), and then do one exercise from this book each week. Take about one to two hours for each "class" session. Rotate between the homes of the various mothers and have a different mother act as group leader each week. If no Leclaire Method instructor or center is available in your area, you can contact us directly for support or visit my Web site at http://www.leclairemethod.com, or E-mail birthing@gte.net.

4. Play your *Hypnosis and Pregnancy* tape at least once each week throughout your pregnancy. During your third trimester, play it three to six times each week. Beginning in week 39, play the labor tape daily.

5. Have a sensual and relaxing pregnancy. Sensual simply means indulging your senses and yourself.

As Jacques Daval wrote long ago, in 1612, "Children in their mother's womb are like tender plants rooting in a garden. They are forced to draw their nourishment from the sap that comes to them there."[2] That much hasn't changed in the process of pregnancy and birth. The Leclaire Method is a guide to help you choose a miraculous beginning for you, your baby, and your family. The focus of this program is on the mind, body, and spirit connections for a healthy and conscious pregnancy. You will learn a systematic approach using holistic techniques for managing your pregnancy, your labor, and your life. It is our privilege and power as women to bring peace to the world one baby at a time.

---

2. As quoted in Jacques Gelis's *History of Childbirth: Fertility, Pregnancy, and Birth in Early, Modern Europe* (Boston: Northeastern University Press, 1991).

Chapter One

ONLY NATURAL

WOMAN'S ABILITY TO BRING NEW LIFE
INTO THE WORLD WITHOUT PAIN

The ability to bring new life into the world is a miracle beyond comprehension, and yet birth is too often viewed as a "medical procedure" and not as a joy-filled event. Growing up as the eldest of nine children in an Irish Catholic neighborhood in New York City, I saw birthing as both an everyday event and a joyous and sacred occasion. When I recall the conversations I heard about childbirth, I do not remember stories of pain and long, hard labors. I remember stories of how much faster this one was than the one before; I remember how much the family's happiness swelled with each successive birth. Women with the most children received the most recognition and respect. Babies were so special that an entire room in the basement of our grand old apartment building, St. Alban's Court, was designated the "carriage room."

When I birthed my own babies, there was no celebratory environment—just a cold, dark hospital room and a bed with side rails. I don't remember how I envisioned the births that took place during my childhood, but it certainly wasn't in the depressing, lonely conditions of a hospital labor room. I think I imagined all the fathers down at the local Irish bar, drinking up a storm, while the "pregnant" father paced or twirled anxiously on the bar stool. When the blessed event occurred, a phone call was made to the pub, a cheer ran through the house, a taxi was called, and the proud father and his cronies piled together into the cab as they drove to meet the newborn Pope or Mother Teresa. There was much joy and hope surrounding birthing. A great miracle happened each time a newborn entered the neighborhood, and the excitement was felt and talked about by all.

These feelings of hope and joy seemed lacking in childbirth as I experienced it and as I observed it as an adult in the tales of friends and clients. Too often, women today do not feel that connection. Instead, they anticipate pain as a part of pregnancy. When women know only fear and associate giving birth with uncontrollable pain, they tend to have more difficult birthing experiences.

The impetus for the Leclaire Method of mind/body–centered pregnancy and pain-free childbirth came, ultimately, from these women I knew in childhood, the women of Our Lady of the Angels and St. John's Parish. It was their joy and excitement I wanted to capture, their sense of the natural ease of bringing babies into the world. Although many women of Our Lady of the Angels and St. John's Parish experienced the same type of birthing that I did—with doctors "delivering" and cold hospital rooms—they also shared in a community of women in which giving birth was "wealth" and they learned from the experiences of others.

Women can easily give birth in comfort and without fear, and the practices in this book will help you do just that. While you are preparing yourself for a comfortable birthing, you can use the same techniques to communicate your love to your baby. You will learn to bond with your baby—and partner—for a healthy and happy family.

RETURN TO A WOMAN-CENTERED APPROACH

Women today are in a wonderful place in many ways. They choose their education and careers, they have the freedom to pursue their dreams, and they create their own businesses and lifestyles. Unfortunately, despite all these advances, women at some point were taken from their active role of birthing babies and asked to assume a more passive role, allowing doctors to "deliver" the baby that came from their own wombs. In this one area, women took a big step backward in 1940, when well-known psychoanalyst Helene Deutsch posed her theory that woman's role during her pregnancy and labor ought to be one of passivity. If the woman took charge of her body, Deutsch said that she would distort her femininity into masculinity and would have complications during birth.[1]

Luckily, women and medical practitioners are growing beyond theories such as Deutsch's. Our bodies know exactly how to birth our babies in a calm, joyous, and loving manner. We now know, in fact, that the body of a woman who renounces her participation in any part of her life and remains a passive bystander responds in many different ways, usually negative. Feelings of prenatal anxiety, feelings of degradation and shame, feelings of being overwhelmed, severe morning sickness, inability to bond with her baby, potential complications, inability to breastfeed, and postpartum depression are some of the possible ways. These symptoms, especially morning sickness, may also be the body trying to put itself back into balance by ridding itself of excess

---

1. In defense of Helene Deutsch, she was a product of the male analytical movement. I almost believe she was trying to belong to that community and thought that if she participated in the oppression of women, she would become one of the guys.

kapha or stagnation. (*Kapha* is an ayurvedic term describing one of the imperfections of the body that can disturb the balance and natural rhythm and cause a heaviness throughout the person, both physical and emotional. The term *ayurvedic* refers to the science of life, which is an ancient Eastern medical tradition.) It is our selves and our own minds now acting under the manifesto of our culture that often get in the way.

In fact, birth is not medicine. It is a natural process, like making love or laughing at a joke. Obstetrics is medicine, and medicine is critical when a mother and child experience complications during birth. Otherwise, a woman and her support team can do better without intrusive instructions or assistance. Since the beginning of human life on Earth, women have helped other women give birth to healthy babies. Midwives are trained to offer advice and support without unnecessary interference. Mothers do the work of birth, not doctors or nurses. Midwives still "catch" more healthy babies worldwide than obstetricians do. (*Catching the baby* is the phrase most often used in the past to describe the process of assisting a mother during labor and childbirth.)

According to the World Health Organization, both midwives and obstetricians have a place in healthy birthing, but midwives and mothers take the predominant roles unless there are problems. "Midwifery is a completely separate health profession which predates obstetrics and which is treated as a separate discipline in nearly every industrialized country in the world," it states. "Midwives practice midwifery care and obstetricians practice obstetrical care and it is clear the best possible maternity care occurs when the women have the benefit of both types of care used appropriately—that is midwifery care for the normal pregnancy and birth and obstetrical care for the complications."

Every pregnant woman needs the support of her obstetrician. During labor and birth, however, mothers, with the aid of midwives and other support people, may create a more natural and pain-free environment to welcome the new life.

THE POWERFUL CONNECTION
BETWEEN MOTHER AND UBORN

The media would have us believe that bonding with a newborn infant begins at that moment when the doctor or midwife hands the baby to the new mother. The latest research demonstrates, however, what many women have long known: that conscious bonding and communication need to begin before you hold your new child in your arms. Whether we know it or not, we communicate feelings and emotions to the babies growing inside us. They eat the same foods we eat and ingest the same vitamins or other chemicals we ingest. In the same way our own bodies "feel" emotions, these feelings pass with our blood into the child. Uborns absorb messages from their mothers, and they experience sounds and other communications while they are in the womb. Mother–infant bonding is a crucial step toward healthy babies, healthy mothers, and a balanced, loving family life. Because of this connection, I speak of *uborn* rather than of *fetus.* Because a baby is already "born" when he is in the uterus, he is born into the uterus and uterine-borne, living in the uterus and carried in the uterus; I call him, therefore, a uborn. The word *uborn* incorporates the unborn child, his sensibility, and his intrauterine environment, including the mother and child's emotional, physical, and spiritual interaction.

For mothers-to-be, communications and bonding begin prior to birth. The months of carrying new life can also be months of connecting with your uborn. Having a role in the growth and development of every life are play, exercise, the social system, and nutrition. As a mother-to-be, you—together with your partner—will want to acknowledge and address each of these areas of development and to nurture all aspects of the new life you have created.

You can learn to connect with and nourish your uborn's amazing developing sense through talking or singing to her, physical nutrition, music, healthy thinking, meditation and relaxation, and physical activity. Throughout this book, success stories of other mothers will illustrate these methods of communication and bonding. By incorporating a few of these practices into your own pregnancy, you will discover how easy it is to use and adapt them to help you.

The Effect of Your Emotions on Your Baby's Well-Being

The way we react to emotional upheavals and conflict today is a result of our past memories. Time after time, uborns have been known to respond to their long-term intrauterine relationship with their mothers by acknowledging her voice, being soothed by her touch, and responding biochemically to her emotions. A study that strikingly manifests this was done with unborn babies and their mothers during the third trimester. (Because the researchers were not certain of the outcome, I shall not judge this first study. I believe, however, that to repeat this study would be evil.)

Pregnant women were asked to rest on their backs and to remain as still as possible for twenty minutes while being filmed by an ultrasound. They were not told that when a mother rests like this, her uborn soon rests quietly, too. When the baby eventually lay still in utero, the mother was told that no movement could be detected on the ultrasound screen. Her baby was no longer moving. The intent of the experiment was to have the mother experience terror in order to measure how quickly her fear produced a reaction in her child. Seconds after each woman was given the information that her child was motionless, the baby sensed the mother's distress and began to kick vehemently. These responses illustrate the power of the mother/uborn mind/body connection during every phase of pregnancy.

The stress response initiated by the mother's body may adversely affect the uborn. Adrenaline may decrease the blood flow to the uterus and the placenta, for example. The womb establishes the child's expectations of his future environment.

Love and nurturing here can lead to emotional stability and loving relationships for the future.

To help you explore your own concerns—including the roller-coaster ride of emotions and ambivalence you might feel right up until you hold your child to your breast—clear, simple steps are presented throughout this book. You yourself can acknowledge any fears and then refocus them into positive thoughts and actions.

I find it exciting that our bodies present to us the symbol of what we need to address in our psyches. Through childbirth, we can grasp all of our dimensions and expand them to participate with the life force. Finally, this emotional and physical stability will be the basis on which mother/child and family bonding build after birth. The healthy foundation allows for continued emotional, physical, and mental health.

Case Study: Sarah

Recently, a friend relayed the following story to me. Sarah is the mother of a teenage daughter, Nina, who is experiencing many difficult emotions, and both mother and daughter are undergoing therapy. Sarah was in her early twenties when she became pregnant with Nina. Although she was married, her marriage was in turmoil, and she and her husband were having difficult times. She was working throughout most of her pregnancy, and as the couple had only one car, her husband agreed to pick her up each evening at 5:30 when she left work. She had to wait in an undesirable part of town, and he was often late. Many times, she waited as much as an hour in the dark before he came. This was a traumatic wait for her, and when he did arrive, even when he was on time, fights and arguments often followed. Exhausted from working, Sarah dreaded these evenings and was happier at work than at home.

After Nina was born, Sarah noticed that she fussed every afternoon before dinner. From about 5:00 until about 6:30, Nina could not be comforted. Eventually, Sarah remembered her troubled waits and the anxiety that she had felt every night before she got off work. As Sarah told me, she had no proof that the baby's fussiness and discomfort were related to her anxious hours during her pregnancy, but it seemed more than a coincidence. Prenatal memories can exert an extraordinary influence on our lives; the postpartum life of an infant is integrally influenced by what happened in utero.

Case Study: Mai

Mai's story is a good example of how our emotions manifest themselves and how doctors often do not have the whole picture. Mai is a busy investment banker, controlling millions of dollars. Mai takes great pride in competing (and usually winning) in a predominantly male marketplace. To her, business is a game, and her competitive spirit and calculating intelligence make her a formidable opponent. Mai's high energy serves her well in this business, and she has an open and playful approach to people.

Mai's obstetrician did not understand why suddenly, during the second trimester, Mai's pregnancy became threatened. He placed her on bed rest, but even then her pregnancy seemed to be in danger. Her health was fine otherwise, and neither the doctor nor Mai could find the reason why she was experiencing premature contractions even though she was following her obstetrician's advice and remaining at home and in bed.

The solution became obvious when I was called to make a home visit during the fifth month of Mai's pregnancy. Mai was on the verge of closing two big deals. When I walked into her spacious home, I was directed to her bedroom—now her office. Here she was, propped up amid a pile of papers, two telephones, a fax machine, and an at-home fetal monitoring device. She was holding court in her room, with a houseman, cook, and maid nearby to run errands and keep the home "office" functioning. In high spirits, she seemed to be enjoying herself.

I laughed as I said to her, "One quick home visit and your OB would see that there is nothing mysterious about your condition. It is exactly as it should be." Neither her body nor her baby could take the stress of her lifestyle. This became obvious with my simple observation of her habits and how she followed "bed rest." Mai was not honoring the needs of her body and of the growing baby for peaceful rest. My job was now to help her align her mind, her body, and her spirit so that she could make realistic choices about eliminating stress from her life.

Until Mai learned to deal with the reality that her baby was intruding on her lifestyle, her pregnancy would remain in jeopardy. Once she could accept the fact that pregnancy and a child would change her life and understand her ambivalence about this change, she could eliminate her physical rejection of it. Being of a pragmatic mind, Mai soon realized what needed to be done and decided to look seriously at the situation at hand and to resolve it to the best of her ability. Mai learned to acknowledge her concerns and moved on to healthy thought processes. I'm happy to say that she held her beautiful baby boy to term—and then some. The fact that Mai's pregnancy extended longer than term may be due to her residual ambivalence about the birth, her reluctance to acknowledge the importance and real significance of this child to her life.

THE EFFECT OF FAMILY DYNAMICS
ON YOUR UBORN

We cannot really say how many times an unborn child can endure stressful emotions before her personality structure is affected. We do know, however, that family dynamics directly influence the uborn and should be taken into consideration. When we recognize this influence, pregnancy can become a time of maternal–paternal–fetal bonding.

In essence, your unborn child is a part of your own mind/body. You are unable to be a passive bystander in your pregnancy and birth. You are a participant in the life of your new baby and pregnancy whether you choose to be or not. When you acknowledge this, you can respond by being proactive rather than reactive. In your womb lies the next generation. In addressing the prenatal life of your uborn, not only will you affect your happiness and your child's, you may also affect adolescent sexual behavior, fertility, disease, and lifestyle, as well as the intellectual, emotional, social, economic, and peaceful development of the world. You have the ability to produce blessings from the nursery rather than ghosts from the past. You have the chance to contribute to a generation of ethical, gentle, caring millennials (a term I use to describe the children of this new millennium). Truly, it is your privilege and power as a woman to bring peace to the world one baby at a time.

A WORD ABOUT SIBLINGS

Often mothers pregnant with their second baby are afraid to bond with the new baby because they fear that bonding may be a violation of their bond with their first child. These mothers don't yet realize that they will love each child equally, just in a different way. If you are pregnant and already have another child (or more), depending on her age, you may invite her to touch your abdomen or to sing to the uborn. You may ask her to do the exercise on drawing in Chapter Two or to draw a picture of the new baby.

WORKING TOGETHER
WITH YOUR PARTNER

Although mothers tend to be willing to deal with most conflicts of pregnancy and motherhood, often they do not seek or receive support from the father. Fathers frequently seem frightened of facing the feelings and fears that emerge. They then withdraw, which triggers the mother's fear of abandonment. In fact, the father's withdrawal is usually triggered by his own fear of abandonment, because he feels left out of the pregnancy. A vicious cycle is created—with both partners afraid of being abandoned and experiencing their greatest fear. What must the innocent ego of the uborn be experiencing as these stress hormones are passed along the umbilical cord? The resolution to this dilemma is simple, but it is not so very easy.

It is important to be who we are. It is important to articulate the myriad feelings arising as a result of pregnancy. These feelings are not unique to any one mother or father; be assured that you are not alone. If you do not speak these feelings, however, you *will be* alone. When you isolate yourself and distance yourself from your mate, you will experience these feelings without support or comfort. There is nothing wrong with keeping some thoughts about your pregnancy to yourself, but do not do so in a hostile way. Be as open, self-searching, and loving as you can be.

When we meet our own needs, it is easier to meet the needs of partners and children. All of these emotions, thoughts, and feelings affect your pregnancy and the onset and outcome of true labor. The purpose of this program is to help you say, as a new mother said to me recently, "I learned that my fears were not bad; they were just the beginning of creating the sunny prospects I wished for. They were as far from the actual experience of birthing as flour and eggs are from a wedding cake, but just as real a possibility."

WHAT MOTHERS BELIEVE ABOUT BIRTH

The way the world views childbirth is a direct reflection of the whole of society. My intent is to change that view. Here is a comparison of the old paradigm with my new ideas.

Old paradigm: I am pregnant.

New paradigm: I am the one who is physically pregnant. My spouse's behavior and our entire environment participate in our pregnancy.

Old paradigm: My body is a separate entity from my uborn. I am merely a babysitter. My uborn will be nourished no matter what.

New paradigm: Any stress experienced by me during pregnancy is felt and metabolized by my uborn. If prolonged, it can create many difficulties in my baby's life. My baby is what I eat, drink, and think.

Old paradigm: There is my mind. There is my body. They are independent of each other.

New paradigm: The thoughts of my mind become chemicals that communicate with all the organs of my body. They are interconnected.

Old paradigm: My thoughts are private. No one is affected by my silent thinking.

New paradigm: My thoughts interact with my uborn's mind/body. There is a positive correlation between unwanted pregnancies and birth defects.

Old paradigm: I am powerless over my thoughts and therefore can have no responsibility for the outcome of my pregnancy.

New paradigm: I can change my negative thoughts to healthy thoughts, and this new thinking will participate in a positive way with my body and my uborn. I have *some* responsibility for the outcomes of my pregnancy.

Old paradigm: There is my pregnancy. There is my labor. There is our birth.

New paradigm: There is a direct correlation between labor and birth outcomes and the way I view pregnancy and prepare myself and my uborn for birth.

MIRACULOUS BEGINNINGS

Birth should be—and is—a beautiful, creative experience for mother, father, infant, and the entire family. The Leclaire Method is designed to provide you with the practical information you need to help your own mind/body, with your natural ability as a woman, to prepare for and give birth. Your body is created to do this miraculous thing, and you can find the joy and excitement of the process with these few simple exercises. I do hope you and your support person enjoy the process of preparing for a creative and joyous birthing.

Chapter Two

THE POWER OF
HEALTHY BELIEFS

TRANSFORMING FEARS INTO CONFIDENCE

Healthy thinking means letting rational thought processes emerge into everyday thinking. It means transforming your fears into rational thoughts. Irrational thinking, myths, and fears can have a negative impact on your pregnancy, your uborn, your labor, and your life. Healthy thinking can have an equally strong positive impact. Transforming fears and creating rational thoughts will take conscious awareness until the process becomes a habit. The exercises later in this chapter, and throughout this book, will help you incorporate healthy thought patterns into your daily life. Throughout the weeks of your pregnancy, you will learn how to achieve physiological, emotional, and spiritual balance with minimal effort.

Many feelings arise spontaneously during pregnancy that cannot be dealt with prior to their emergence. When they do arise, the mother's willingness to deal with them rather than deny them is crucial. Labor is probably one of the most thought-about and anxiety-producing aspects of pregnancy, and later in this book you will learn more about what I call "zen and the art of labor."

You will continue the roller-coaster ride of ambivalence throughout your pregnancy. No one can control all of her feelings and emotions, of course, nor should you try. *Moments of fear will not do permanent damage to your child or you.* Prolonged fears or stress, or unacknowledged negative emotions, however, may have a negative impact. How you react to those fears can have a profound impact on your health. These exercises are designed to help you acknowledge your concerns and fears, but to avoid letting those feelings control you.

THE RATIONAL THOUGHT PROCESS
FOR HEALTHY THINKING

The Rational Thought Process (RTP) is based on the method of achieving instant happiness developed by the internationally known Maxie Maultsby, M.D., professor of psychiatry at Howard University. In 1987, I had the good fortune of working with Dr. Maultsby and learning this method from him at the Simonton Cancer Center. He taught this method to many people, some of whom were patients afraid of dying. They were able to use RTP immediately to turn fear into serenity. This process has also worked for many pregnant women, helping them to respond rationally rather than emotionally to their fears.

To see how this works, let's look at another situation in which a response to fears might be emotional rather than rational. Imagine a day at the beach. The water is calm. There isn't a swell in sight. There's a gentle breeze. The sun is at its zenith. The water feels cool and delightful, and you do not have a care in the world. You decide to go out onto the water in a rubber raft, to float with the waves and dream. You feel marvelous, totally relaxed and content. All of a sudden, you see people rushing from the water onto the beach, and you hear the lifeguard shouting through his megaphone, "Everyone out of the water. SHARKS!"

What would happen next? How would you feel? What would you do? You would probably feel terrified and rush from the water as quickly as possible.

Stop for a moment and think about what caused your fear and your reactions. The shark didn't; you didn't even see the animal. What caused your fear was your belief in the lifeguard's words and your own belief system about sharks. Our body doesn't know that it is reacting to our belief system and not to an actual shark, however. The fear creates a chemical pathway that sends a message from our brain to our body. Thus, our mind has projected itself into our body, causing our body to react or interact.

EXERCISE: THE RATIONAL THOUGHT PROCESS

Now let's look at how the rational thought process can help us transform our fears into rational beliefs and plans of action.

To begin this exercise, list four beliefs that you have surrounding labor. To help you understand, here is an example. Following are four possible beliefs about pregnancy, labor, and childbirth:

1. Childbirth is intensely painful. The pain will be so unbearable that I'll need an epidural.

2. I won't be able to push my baby out with an epidural.

3. I'll end up having a cesarean section.

4. I can do nothing about any of this. I am a helpless victim.

Now write down your own four beliefs on a sheet of paper and set them aside as you continue to read.

We need to correct our attitudes and our myths rather than have them imposed on us. The following questions can help you evaluate your beliefs to determine if they are rational or irrational. Review the beliefs you just wrote down and evaluate them based on these criteria:

- Are my thoughts, emotions, feelings, and physical reactions based on obvious fact?

- Do my thoughts best help me to protect my life and health and the health of my baby?

- Do my current thoughts best help me to achieve my long-term and short-term goals?

- Do my thoughts best help me to avoid my most undesirable interactions?
- Do my thoughts best help me to feel the emotions I want to feel?

Keep these five questions handy, and whenever you slip into old, unhealthy thought patterns, feelings, or behaviors, stop yourself, find privacy (a bathroom will do), and talk to yourself about these patterns. Work through each of the questions as they relate to your feelings, and then take the following steps:

1. Elaborate on the *unhealthy beliefs*.
2. Change them into *healthy* beliefs.
3. Formulate an *affirmation* incompatible with each unhealthy belief.
4. Develop a *plan of action* that will move you in the direction of your desired goal.

Now read how a woman named Catherine transformed the four fears listed at the beginning of this exercise into goal-oriented, rational beliefs, affirmations, and plans of action. Catherine went on to deliver a beautiful baby girl vaginally.

Belief One

Unhealthy belief: Childbirth is intensely painful. The pain will be so unbearable that I'll need an epidural.

Healthy belief: I may or may not have severe pain, and what I do will make a significant difference.

Affirmation: My contractions, which I'll think of as rhythmic risings of my uterus, at some point will be intense, and that is good. It will mean that my uterus is working efficiently to push my baby down through the birth canal. I shall participate by relaxing. If I do feel pain, it is just a message that I need to relax more deeply. I intend to have all the emotional support that I need during my pregnancy and labor, from my spouse, family, friends, midwife, physician, doula, or a professional support person I hire to be there just for me.

Plan of action: I'll listen to my *Hypnosis and Pregnancy* tape three times this week. I'll learn other tools for minimizing pain.

Belief Two

Unhealthy belief: I won't be able to push my baby out with an epidural.

Healthy belief: If I do initially have an epidural, I can let it wear off right before it is time for me to push my baby out.

Affirmation: If I relax sufficiently and remain ambulatory for as long as possible and explore many different positions, I probably will be able to do without an epidural.

Plan of action: I'll exercise at least three times each week throughout my pregnancy by walking, swimming, or doing yoga. I'll play my *Hypnosis and Pregnancy* tape at least three times a week and my *Hypnosis for Labor* tape at week 39 and as soon as I begin the first stage of labor. I'll play it again as soon as I am settled in my birthing room. I'll have at least one support person who knows my labor and birth plan and is willing to support me in it. I'll do all the work in this book and meditate at least three or four times each week for twenty minutes, and I'll listen to my *Leclaire Smart Beginnings Music* tape. If I have an epidural, I will aim toward letting it wear off as I reach the end of the first stage of labor so I can feel to push when the time comes. I'll play my *Leclaire Smart Beginnings Music* tape as soon as I have an epidural and will continue to play it when the epidural wears off, if I choose.

Belief Three

Unhealthy belief: I'll end up having a cesarean section.

Healthy belief: I may or may not have a cesarean section, and what I do makes a significant difference.

Affirmation: If I exercise during my pregnancy and learn to relax my mind, body, and spirit; if I practice good nutrition; if I avoid harmful substances; if I choose a supportive midwife or doctor and do all the work in this book and practice with my *Hypnosis and Pregnancy* and *Smart Beginnings Music* tapes at least three times each week, I will probably not need a cesarean section. If for some unforeseen reason I do need one, I will at least know that I did the best that I could do and that my new attitudes and beliefs can now play a positive role in my recovery.

Plan of action: I'll do research before I choose a midwife and doctor or a hospital birthing center. I'll find out their statistics regarding cesarean sections, and I'll then make the most intelligent decision possible. If I need a cesarean section, I'll play my *Meditation and Healing* tape so I will heal easily and quickly. I'll be gentle with myself. I'll be grateful that I am healthy and that my baby is healthy.

Belief Four

Unhealthy belief: I can do nothing about any of this. I am a helpless victim. All of my unhealthy beliefs will increase my pain and will keep my cervix from effacing and dilating. This in turn will lengthen my labor and could create a medical emergency, and I can do nothing about this.

Healthy belief: All of my unhealthy beliefs and feelings are making me worse, and I want to change them. Other people have changed their belief systems. It was possible for them, and it is possible for me, too. My fears are great but not insurmountable.

Affirmation: I give myself permission to change my unhealthy beliefs. I will do all the work that it takes to change my unhealthy beliefs.

Plan of action: I will spend my pregnancy taking good care of myself, relaxing, and being compassionate toward myself and my uborn. I'll take time each week to play. I'll spend time daily meditating. (See Chapter Four.) I'll spend at least five minutes five days each week holding and being held by my husband or partner. At this time, we'll turn off the television and telephone, and we'll talk about nothing upsetting. Maybe we won't talk at all. (Such times are good for playing your *Smart Beginnings Music* tape and just being with each other, caressing and fondling in a caring and loving way. This will fulfill your bonding needs, not necessarily your sexual needs.)

Now transform *your* unhealthy beliefs into healthy new ones by completing the entire exercise. You may be saying to yourself that this is easier said than done. Creating new myths, whether about labor and childbirth or about your daily routine, takes practice just as relaxation or meditation takes practice. Keep this paper with your new beliefs handy and read them to yourself daily for five days. Then read them anytime you begin to feel afraid. You have now begun to prepare yourself physically and mentally; you have taken the first steps to prevent fetal and maternal distress. Ask your support person to make his own list, and share your lists with each other. Be loving, supportive, and understanding—never critical—of each other as you share your fears. This increases parental bonding and fulfills a need that you each have at this time for loving, caring support.

Case Study: Kathleen

To understand that examining your feelings and facing them can help you, look for a moment at the problem of a mother named Kathleen. Kathleen came into therapy when she was seventeen weeks pregnant. She had been experiencing severe nausea and vomiting, which was beginning to subside. She had been raped when she was in college and was so shamed by the experience that she had never discussed it with anyone in her family. Her husband, James, had no knowledge of her horrible experience. It became imperative for Kathleen to discuss this horrific happening while she was pregnant. She felt guilty and dishonest, as though she had violated her marriage and wasn't deserving of real serenity and happiness. She felt that her husband rightly honored his mother more than he did Kathleen. After all, she thought, how could James respect her after she had been brutally sexually violated? The damage was engraved on her being.

Through individual therapy and the Rape Crisis Center, Kathleen was able to let go of much of her negativity. Her relationship with her husband and her mother-in-law improved, and her relationship with herself and her uborn became one of calm acceptance.

PICTURES WORTH A THOUSAND WORDS

How a woman feels about pregnancy and childbirth directly correlates to how she will experience pregnancy and childbirth. It is thus imperative that the mother learn to deal with her conflicting attitudes about marriage, pregnancy, birthing, motherhood, breastfeeding, and her career. She needs to attend to these in order to prevent displacement of these feelings into a physical resistance manifested by anxiety, fear, pain, and even maternal and/or fetal distress.

I have discovered that one of the most effective ways in which mothers and fathers can revise their ideas about birth and labor is by drawing simple pictures to illustrate their thoughts about birth. Often they can express their ideas better through these images than through words. Take a few moments now to do the following exercise. You will need a large sheet of blank paper and some crayons, colored pencils, or markers. If all you have is a pencil, use that. (Alternatively, you may choose to do a collage of cut pictures glued onto a large sheet of paper.) You'll be amazed at what you learn.

EXERCISE: DRAWING

Both mother-to-be and partner and/or support person should take some time to do this exercise during the first trimester of pregnancy and then redo it during the second and third trimesters. Spend some time during each trimester discussing your attitudes without judging either yourself or your partner. Remain open and curious.

STEP 1A *(for mother-to-be):* Draw a picture of your body and your baby. Include in this picture anything in your life that you see as a possible source of worry to you and anything that you feel might act as a deterrent to your having the most joyous pregnancy/birthing possible.

Do the drawing as quickly and as spontaneously as you can, with as little deliberation as possible. Have fun, and play with it. Allow yourself to be free and honest. This is not a test of your artistic ability. If you don't want to draw, do a collage, again choosing whatever suits your fancy. Make the drawing or collage a free association. Give yourself permission to surprise yourself, if that is what your unconscious is trying to do. You do not have to be afraid of what emerges, as we only allow ourselves to see that which we are ready to look at. Take a risk. It can do you no harm, and it is possible that great good can come to you when you break through some of your denial. In the next section, you'll see some samples.

STEP 1B *(for support person):* Draw a picture, or do a collage, of your partner and her baby. Draw a picture, or do a collage, of yourself in relation to them. Include in the picture anything about pregnancy or parenthood that you find exciting, fearsome, or anxiety producing. Read the mother's exercise and follow the same pattern of openness as is suggested to her.

STEP 2: Answer the following questions about your drawings. Be honest.

- What are three things that you like about your drawing?
- What are three things that you don't like?
- What would you like to change about your drawing?

STEP 3: Now make a chart as follows. List both the positive and negative feelings evoked by your own illustrations in relation to various aspects of your relationship, your pregnancy, your life, and your new baby:

Positive Feelings	Negative/Ambivalent Feelings
Marriage	
Pregnancy	
Labor	
Birthing	
Parenting	
Breastfeeding	
Career	

STEP 4: Share your drawing and your feelings with someone you trust and spend some time discussing these issues. In order to feel happier in your daily life, how do you need to change your thinking, your attitudes, your beliefs, and your behavior around the negative or ambivalent feelings you have listed? Your feelings will follow.

Drawings and Their Stories

I have used this exercise many times to help fathers and mothers express their concerns about the mother's body, their uborn, the father's feelings, and any external situations that may be interfering with a healthy relationship between father, mother, and uborn. Many things come through in these drawings that mothers and fathers don't always articulate in words. You'll learn from this process, and after you've gone through the entire book and practiced the exercises, your drawings will reflect a new peace and confidence.

One father, when doing this exercise, drew himself trying to crawl inside his wife's uterus with the uborn. "I want to be safe inside, also," he declared. "He has it made, all curled up in there. I have to worry about being the caretaker of everyone. I wish I could just be curled up inside the safety of the amniotic fluid." This father was, in fact, a very nurturing husband and was also very supportive to the other fathers in the group. He went on to

FIGURE 1

face his fears and to be a supportive presence during his wife's labor. He was the caretaker he needed to be.

Another father drew himself physically supporting his wife (figure 1) and then decided this was how he wished he could be, rather than how he was able to be. He was afraid of losing his wife as a playmate, friend, and lover. He then began to discuss his fear of fainting when the baby's head crowned. His wife drew herself taking care of herself (figure 2). She had been taking care of herself separately from her classes with her husband. After much discussion, a decision was made that the father would be his wife's support person up to the time when the baby's head crowned, and then he would leave her with her second support person. Prior to drawing the picture, this couple had been having increased arguments. After they discussed the father's fears and came to an agreement, the arguing subsided, and the father was able to return to being a nurturing figure for his wife. After a few private sessions, mother and father graciously accepted and understood each other's wishes. She decided to have the birth

Figure 2

she wanted no matter how he behaved. She came weekly to discuss her feelings and dreams, and she meditated, exercised, and listened to her tapes. She did have the birth she wanted. Her husband witnessed the entire labor and birth. When he became anxious, he sat in a chair and observed quietly.

Other drawings helped mothers and support persons both to understand and to work with their feelings. Figure 3 shows a uborn in the posterior position and in the proper position for birth. Mother Kim did this drawing of her uborn Karin in her thirty-seventh week of pregnancy. (See Chapter Twelve for the full story.) Kim's uborn was in the wrong position for birth, and this concerned Kim. She wanted a vaginal birth. She used the drawing to express how she saw the situation and to suggest to Baby Karin a better position. Figure 4 shows the uborn's face as it was at the time and as it should be for delivery.

One mother drew a picture of her pregnant self with all sorts of images and words surrounding her: telephone, schoolwork, a ticking clock, a heart with a man's name, a house, children she

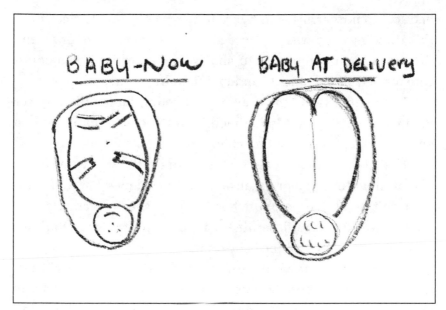

FIGURE 3

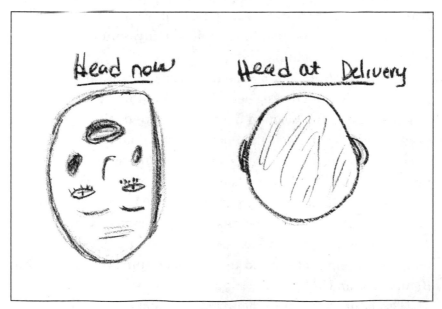

FIGURE 4

had lost to miscarriages in figure 5. Her worries were clear from this drawing: She was not sure she would have time for all the things she had committed to and was wondering if she could care for herself and a child and maintain her relationship.

The mother titled the drawing "Eugenia Contemplating Her Pregnancy, Birth, and Motherhood." On the one hand, it felt like an execution of sorts. On the other, it was mystical and magical.

The father who drew figure 6 was afraid that his wife would yell at him during labor because he didn't know what to do and wouldn't be able to support her the way she wanted. He was afraid the baby would be hit by a car and afraid he wouldn't know what to do when the baby cried.

Figure 7 was drawn by a mother afraid that she might not breathe during labor, because she sometimes had asthmatic attacks when she was anxious. She did not trust her intuition that she would know when to push or be quiet. The drawing also depicts her concerns over which position would be best for her (floor, bed, chair) and that the hospital staff would make her "go to bed" like a little child.

Tom, who drew figure 8, could focus only on the trip to the hospital. Living in Los Angeles, all he could think about was getting his wife to the hospital once labor started. He couldn't see beyond the freeway, so he had no other fears or anxieties. All his attention was focused on the "concrete." (The couple made it on time and now have a healthy baby.)

The artistic father who drew figure 9 said, "We'll fly together,"—but the picture reveals his huge concerns about money.

One mother did a collage with a drawing of a uborn in the womb on a flap that opened to whales jumping and swimming (figures 10a and 10b).

The father who drew figure 11 had some worries but also seemed confident that they could meet those concerns.

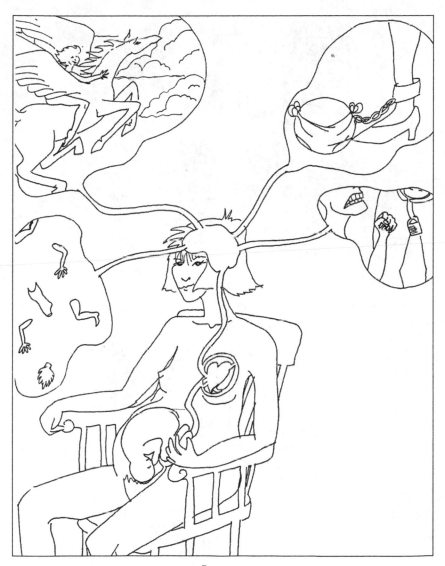

FIGURE 5

FIGURE 6

FIGURE 7

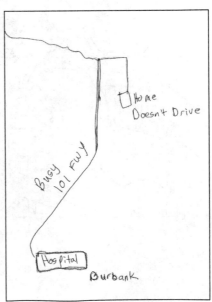

FIGURE 8

FIGURE 9

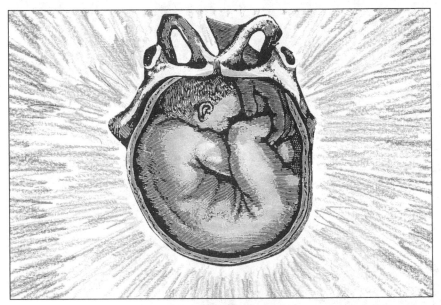

FIGURE 10a

FIGURE 10b

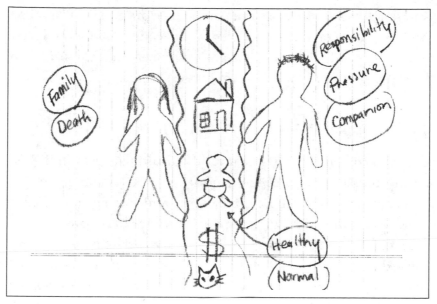

FIGURE 11

COMING TO TERMS
WITH FEARS AND CONCERNS

A pictorial story of pregnancy and the fears and desires surrounding it often reveals the hidden contents of our minds. Once these become consciously present, they can be organized to create the outcomes we desire. This kind of psychological preparation can help both the mother and the father to shape their desired outcomes. When you explore the images and observe your drawings, you will receive information about yourself that you may not have been able to process before. Drawing the pictures gives mothers and fathers time to reflect, and the physical act of drawing also seems to give permission for some of the unacknowledged feelings and emotions to arise and be expressed. At the time of drawing, they are doing—not observing or trying to understand. The discussion and the analysis later provide time to be the observer and to talk about the fears and emotions expressed. This method can also help you to work through your feelings and fears, better preparing you for labor and birth. Here you get in touch first with your doing ego and then with your observing ego.

Taking Responsibility for a Good Birth

All good education brings us toward our ultimate goal in life: an ability to exercise all of the faculties we have been given. We need to train our minds, our bodies, and our spirits. If each mother accepts individual responsibility for herself and, along with that acceptance, takes the initiative to act—that is, to move toward a pregnancy and childbirth the way they were intended to be—she can experience a celebration of life. Many women with whom I have worked have participated with great courage and have embraced a wonderful feeling of freedom and accomplishment through the birthing process.

At the beginning of the twentieth century, a woman who experienced pain in childbirth was rendered unconscious. Today it is becoming apparent that the more aware a woman is, the more comfortable she will be during childbirth. Exploring your fears before labor will help you remain conscious and without pain. The more we take control of our bodies, our selves, and our lives, the less we shall suffer on every plane. Unconsciousness means loss of awareness, and loss of awareness means an inability to experience the great joy and miracle of childbirth.

Case Study: Olivia

One mother, Olivia, realized that her greatest fear of labor was that she would not be seen as innocent and virginal. When she had become pregnant, she had felt a bit embarrassed and tried to minimize her growing uborn and her growing abdomen for quite a while. She was married, and the baby was very much planned and desired.

When she explored this, she recalled riding in the front seat of a family friend's car when she was eight years old as he was taking her and his children for ice cream. He had proceeded to insert his finger in her vagina. She had felt helpless and powerless, somehow that her innocence and virginity were affected. At that time, she hadn't consciously realized that she was beginning to develop an inner awareness of herself as a judging observer. "You are no longer innocent," she chided herself.

On some unconscious level, Olivia looked on herself as not socially acceptable because of her experience with the "ice cream man." She began to feel and believe that labor and breastfeeding are animalistic. She believed that a lady would be silent during birth, wouldn't perspire, wouldn't spread her legs, would in effect just cough; while covering her mouth with a soft and delicate handkerchief, she would, in one gentle push, have her baby. In contrast, a woman would birth in the most comfortable position for her. She would make any sound she needed to facilitate the birthing process. She would wear comfortable clothes for herself or would wear no clothes at all. She wouldn't care at all what people thought of her as she birthed, since she would be so focused in the moment that she wouldn't be thinking, only being. Through discussion, imagery, and hypnosis, Olivia was able to integrate the way a lady would birth, the way a woman would birth, and the mindfulness of animals' birth. She chose a cat. In the coherence of these three different contexts, she was able to come up with imagery that worked for her. She also had to explain to her physician (a male) her fears about labor. We discussed another mother who needed to wear cotton leggings and a big T-shirt in order to feel comfortable. She could visualize her birthing outfit. She realized that squatting was a good position and wanted to do that but felt it was too animalistic. We squatted together and discussed the benefits of both the squatting position and learning from animals.

Olivia became aware of her unhealthy imagery. She also had mindful dialogues about what she felt was necessary to change about this imagery for an easy, psychologically and physically comfortable vaginal birth. This combination helped her create both a new visualization of herself and a new relationship to her own inner dialogue about herself at the time as a pregnant mother and herself as a child in relation to the "ice cream man." It was important for Olivia to return in her mind to the scene and change it.

In doing this, she came up with a new image of the molestation, telling herself the following: After we got out of the car, I got to a telephone booth, and I called my parents from the ice cream store. I told them what happened. I then called the police and said I am here with a man who just molested me, and I am scared, and I don't want to get back in the car with him. My parents and the police came at about the same time. My father punched the man, and the police handcuffed him and arrested him.

For Olivia, imagery had engaged the right hemisphere (the intuitive function of the brain) to alter and process the left brain (analytical) material. After this process, I did a hypnosis with Olivia and replayed the new and more empowering scene. This helped to integrate the interhemispheric resolution of the trauma.

EXERCISE: ACKNOWLEDGING FEARS

Here is another exercise that can help you explore the reasons for your feelings and actions. Both mother and father should do this exercise.

- Make a list of the fears you had as a child that you still have today.

- Make a list of the fears you had as an adolescent that you still have today.

- Make a list of prepregnancy adult fears.

- Make a list of the fears that have come into being since pregnancy began.

- Make a list of the fears that you are aware of that your mother and father may have had or talked about.

- Make a list of the fears that you believe your partner may have.

Decide what fears you are willing to live with and what fears you want to discard. Now make a decision to do whatever work is necessary to eliminate, diminish, or accept certain fears. Decide which fears you do not want to pass on to your child.

After you examine these fears, you may decide to seek professional help to deal with them before they do damage. This is the healthy thing to do, and there is no shame in finding support and help from others.

Chapter Three

ACCEPTING THE MAGIC
OF YOUR MIND

THE HYPNOSIS OF THE LECLAIRE METHOD

The center of the Leclaire Method is to keep the mind out of the body's way so that the body can do its work, and this requires psychological, spiritual, and emotional preparation. Once some of that work has been done, you can let go and allow yourself to be hypnotized, making your labor easy and nearly pain free. Hypnosis for labor and birth is a state of deep concentration of your mind and deep relaxation of your body, which permits the easy passage of your baby through your gradually widening birth canal. Your mind and body can do amazing things, and when we take the time to observe and remain mindful of what they can do, we can harness that power to give the baby a magic carpet ride from womb to mother's arms. For these reasons, I hope you'll take the time to learn these techniques of hypnosis for pregnancy and labor.

The word *hypnosis* derives from the name of the Greek god of sleep, Hypno. It conveys the idea of the ease and rest of sleep, of letting go and allowing the body to do its natural work. Hypnosis also enhances the progress of your labor and allows you to positively participate and calmly assist in the birth of your baby.

With hypnosis, you can easily get through labor without chemical anesthesia. The choice is always yours, of course: You may ask for and receive drugs if you like. Be aware, though, that new evidence indicates that children of mothers who receive opiate derivatives during labor have a higher incidence of drug abuse later in life. In contrast, mothers who experience severe pain and feel out of control can later in life experience an increase in suicidal ideation. In contrast, hypnosis gives you full control.

The Leclaire Method of preparation is the best anesthetic for optimal short- and long-term benefits of pain relief and continued emotional serenity for both mother and baby. The hypnosis of the Leclaire Method offers demedicalization of labor and birth by creating a natural physical anesthesia in the mother. This allows her natural and instinctive ability to birth her baby to become manifest. Hypnosis also allows the mother to move about freely in a comfortable, natural manner. She is able to change her position as needed, which in turn increases her comfort and facilitates the progress of her baby's birth.

It is important for you to begin preparing for birth by playing your *Hypnosis and Pregnancy* tape (see Resources at the back of this book) throughout your pregnancy. Practice will increase your confidence in your ability to imagine desired outcomes and to relax deeply. By preparing early in pregnancy, you will foster your expectancy for a comfortable, easy pregnancy, labor, and birth.

The Leclaire Method is your baby's inherent way to come into your world, and it is your inherent right to believe that you can have a healthy, comfortable birth. You do not have to learn how to birth comfortably. You only have to be allowed to do what is the nature of your body—that is, to progress through labor unrestrained by chemical anesthesia, unrestrained by confinement to bed, unrestrained by continuous electronic fetal monitoring, unrestrained by the beliefs of the medical culture. All you need to do is to remember, silently, to reconnect to your nature. It is your body's nature to know how to respond to your contractions, and it is the nature of your body to know when to push. If chemical anesthesia or the direction of others (except in a medical emergency) takes away your sensations, you are not honoring yourself. We have the right to vote; we have the right to work; we must now have the right to squat and move about freely during labor and to follow our bodies' instinctive wisdom to know when to push.

Hypnosis is your baby's easy way out. This chapter presents a hypnosis script for you to use throughout your pregnancy. Read it to yourself, make a tape for yourself, or have your support person read it to you. Don't feel obligated to try to memorize this or to ask your support person to memorize it or even to fully understand every aspect of it. Just read it through now, ask your support person to do the same, and then mark this page. Then have the book handy to read again during labor. My experience suggests that if the support person reads the script once during the course of your pregnancy and then uses it whenever needed during pregnancy (read from this book or whatever is comfortable), it will help both the mother-to-be and the support person. (Most mothers also choose to use the tape I have prepared. To offer variety, it is different from the following script.)

Although you may find parts of this script odd to read through, read it through anyway. Then read it through again (or have your support person read it to you) or listen to your *Hypnosis and Pregnancy* tape at least once each week throughout your pregnancy, increasing to three to six times each week during your third trimester. Once you've experienced the script, you may have a few questions about what hypnosis is and why I recommend it to mothers. Later in this chapter, I'll answer frequently asked questions, and you'll learn more about why this script can help you with your baby's easy way out. For now, though, let's look at the script itself.

HYPNOSIS FOR PREGNANCY: A SCRIPT

Get yourself into a comfortable position and begin to observe what is in front of you. Now take a deep breath through your nose, filling your abdomen with air. Feel it blowing up like a balloon. Good. Now, as slowly as you possibly can, exhale through your mouth and send the breath all the way down your spine. Now, just focus on your next three exhalations. Don't alter them in any way; just observe them. Well done . . .

Now, contract your feet and your ankles and gently release them. Contract your calves, your shins, and your knees . . . and relax them. Take another deep breath in through your nose . . . and exhale as slowly as you can through your mouth, sending the breath into your right big toe.

Contract your thighs, and then relax them. Inhale through your nose; exhale as slowly as you can through your mouth, sending your breath into your left big toe. Focus on your exhalations. Now turn your attention to your abdomen, placing your hands gently on your belly. Silently explain to your uborn what you are doing and why you are doing this. Now become aware of any feelings that you may be holding in your belly. Label these feelings as a point of reference, not in judgment. Make a decision to deal with these feelings later. For now, take a deep healing breath and breathe all of these feelings (that may disturb you) out of your abdomen.

They have no place in a body that is trying to relax. Inhale deeply and breathe out, sending your disturbing feelings way out into the universe . . . Again, take a deep, healing breath and release your feelings, sending them way out into the universe . . .

Now contract your chest and your shoulders and relax them. Now take your arms, cross them, and rest them gently on your chest. Place your hands gently on your breasts and begin visualizing your breasts nourishing your healthy baby; your milk flows freely, and your baby latches on and suckles well and easily . . . Now contract your right arm, and your left arm. Make a fist with your hands, and now extend them and let them relax and fall wherever they are comfortable.

Now contract your spine until your entire back is arched with tension . . . and release it. Good. Take a deep healing breath and send it all the way down your spine . . . Contract your face, your jaw, scrinch it up like a prune . . . and now open your mouth and your eyes as wide as you can. Stick out your tongue and try to touch your chin with your tongue. Imagine that you are an animal in the wild and that you are releasing your energy through a grand stretch of your body and a great release of sound from deep in your being. Practice your sounding now. (Sounding during labor could use the vowels or the mantras explained in Chapter Nine.)

The mother makes these controlled sounds, which can facilitate the birth through resonating in various parts of her body as the baby moves through the birth canal. It helps to practice these sounds, to avoid screaming or out-of-control sound.) *The more you practice sounding before labor, the more comfortable it will be for you during labor. It is part of your nature to make wonderful, contributing sounds to the birth of your baby.*

Now feel your entire body letting go to the force of gravity. Now imagine yourself climbing down a safe and sturdy wooden staircase that leads you to your own personal healing place, a birthing place. It is a lovely, late spring day. The temperature is perfect. It is midday, and the sun is almost directly overhead. There is a gentle breeze, and you can hear the soft sounds of nature. Enjoy the sounds. Now, keeping your eyes gently closed (after you read this to yourself, do it again from memory with your eyes closed), *focus on your eye and eye socket. What do you see as you look at your closed eyelids? Now create a perfect birthing place in nature through your sense of sight alone. Note the colors, the patterns, the shapes, the movement, the stillness.*

Now become aware of your nose; inhale and experience the air as you draw it into your nostrils. Now become aware of the scents and fragrances in your natural birthing place. Let them comfort and soothe you. Now become aware of your mouth, your lips, teeth, gums, mucous membrane lining of your mouth, your tongue and your throat, your saliva. Imagine luscious fruits growing in your natural birthing place. Begin to taste the rich, full, juicy taste of your own birthing fruit. This fruit will help you carry your healthy baby to full term. At delivery, your birthing fruit will help you to dilate easily, readily, and to allow you to have an easy, comfortable vaginal birth. Now become aware of your ears and all the convolutions of your ears. Become aware of the distant sounds and then the closer sounds, listening to only those sounds and being aware of nothing else but the sound of your breath and all the other sounds around you. Allow any sound that enters into your consciousness to deepen your relaxation; allow any sound that enters into your consciousness to deepen your concentration and focus.

Listen now to the sounds of nature that you hear in your birthing place or healing place. Enjoy those sounds. Let them comfort you and soothe you. Now experience your body in your birthing place. Feel your skin and your clothes, if you are wearing any. Feel the air, the current, and the warmth or the coolness. Feel the textures. You are more and more comfortable. Now experience your birthing place through all of your senses. See it, smell the fragrances, taste the fruits or the clear fresh water. Feel the air, the currents, and the coolness or warmth, the textures, the comfort of your entire being. Now focus your breath, observing both your inhalations and your exhalations but not altering them in any way. All will be silent while you do this. As you inhale silently, say to yourself, "so"; on your exhalation, silently say to yourself, "hum." On the "so," you are inhaling the life force of the universe, and on the "hum," you are exhaling your ego-bound limitations. So, hum.

(Remain quiet for three minutes; then count the mother down.) *"Ten," and down deeper, "nine," deeper and deeper, "eight," down deeper, descending into your own boundless state of well-being, "seven," down, deeper and down, doubling your relaxation. "Six," down, and deeper, now down deeper; double your relaxation, "five," and down, and "four," deeper, and down again, doubling your relaxation. "Three," letting go even more; you are safe and centered, and you have again doubled your relaxation. "Two," and down, and deeper, and "one," and deeper and deeper and down.*

Inhale. Begin to visualize the rest of your pregnancy exactly the way you want it to be. Relax your breath. Inhale. Begin to visualize your first stage of labor at term exactly the way you want it to be. You are moving about, comfortable, relaxed. Relax your breath and inhale. Begin to visualize your active labor at term exactly the way you want it to be. You move your position for your comfort. You easily use sounding. Your hands and your jaw are completely relaxed. You are completely in the moment. Relax your breasts.

Inhale. Begin to visualize your birth at term exactly the way you want it to be. Easy vaginal birth, stretching comfortably, knowing when to push. Relax your breath.

Inhale. Begin to visualize your postpartum exactly the way you want it to be. Your healthy baby is in your arms, the placenta arrives, there is little or no bleeding, and you are all joyous together.

Inhale. You will also naturally know the best position for pushing, and you will know when and how to push your baby out with ease. You will have the energy for your labor/work. It will be enjoyable and engaging. Your healthy baby who you just easily pushed out is now safely in your arms and at your breast. Your perineum is relaxed, and the placenta arrives; there is little or no bleeding, and, as before, you are all joyous together.

Inhale. Now focus on your breath, just observing it and not altering it in any way. With every breath, you go deeper and deeper and down deeper and deeper, deeper now, down and down and deeper. You are at your own center, your place of complete silence within . . .

Now, take the middle finger of your left hand and make a circle on your chest. This is your anchor. Anytime you make this circle once on your chest, you will immediately be able to focus on the task at hand. The more you make the circle on your chest, the more deeply into a trance you will go. When you are deep enough for you, just relax your hand wherever it falls and is comfortable. This will work for you anytime you use it. Of course, you would never use this anchor technique if you were the driver of a moving vehicle.

Now repeat all of the preceding exercise while listening to your Leclaire Smart Beginnings Music *tape (see Resources). Listening increases the learning process by allowing other parts of your brain to be reached than were reached while you did the exercise without music.*

At term, your cervix will easily, comfortably, and progressively efface and dilate, and your baby will continue to move down through the birth canal. The stronger your contractions, the more deeply you will relax. You will participate one contraction at a time. You will be able to find the proper position for yourself as your labor easily progresses. You will be able to rest or meditate deeply between each contraction. With every contraction, you will double your relaxation, concentration, and focus. You will remain comfortable and confident throughout your labor and birth. You will naturally know when to "so" and when to "hum."

HYPNOSIS FOR PREGNANCY AND LABOR

Now that you've tried one sample hypnosis and imagery, you may have a few questions about hypnosis for pregnancy and labor. Hypnosis is connected to relearning your approach to labor and also to letting your body do what it already knows how to do by getting the mind out of its way.

When you hear something that strikes you as funny, you laugh spontaneously; you don't ask yourself how to laugh. In the same way, your body can give birth and provide oxygen for you and your baby. Through training with hypnosis, you will be so prepared that you will automatically and spontaneously breathe correctly during all the stages of labor, and other parts of the labor process will seem equally natural to you.

What a relief! When mothers realize that this is possible, they begin to let go of some of their fears and move toward a greater trust in their own bodies. After all, our bodies do know exactly how to birth our babies. All we need to do is to keep our mind out of the way of our body in doing the work it knows so well and naturally how to do. It really is that simple. Just like walking or breathing, the first step is awareness, understanding, acceptance, and letting go of resistance. The second step is practice, practice, practice.

Through this program of training in hypnosis, the brain is being taught to receive relearning stimuli. At some point, you are pretty much unaware of what is going on around you. The great benefit derived from using hypnosis during childbirth is that it enhances and normalizes the natural physiology of labor and birth by reducing tension. The hypnotic state helps to maintain and assure the *flow* of oxygen to the uborn. Hypnosis eliminates the anxiety that can cause diminished oxygen flow.

You may be wondering whether you will be hypnotized by someone else or if this is self-hypnosis. In fact, all hypnosis is self-hypnosis. Anyone who is "helping" with hypnosis acts as a facilitator, helping you focus on the instructions—but you do the work, and you control the hypnotic state.

Hypnosis is, in fact, nothing more than the state immediately preceding sleep. Through hypnosis, we are able to prolong this state and to enjoy it for an extended period of time if and when necessary. Because hypnosis is a naturally occurring state that all people experience right before falling asleep, everyone can be hypnotized. Not all people will allow themselves to be hypnotized, however, and many people are resistant to being hypnotized.

OVERCOMING RESISTANCE

Although most women are very open to learning hypnosis and visualization techniques and are eager to receive the benefits, some are naturally more receptive than others.

Some women at first feel a resistance to accepting the state of hypnosis. If this is your situation, the first step for you is to understand why you resist. These resistances will usually be brought into consciousness through a dream. If this occurs, you can work through the dream with your midwife or analyst. (See Chapter Seven.)

Like the midwife or doctor, the analyst will aid in facilitating the birth process. Neither the doctor nor the midwife delivers the baby. The baby is birthed by the mother. The Leclaire facilitator becomes better at helping the mother to induce hypnosis when she is in a trance or in a relaxed state. At this time she is more in touch with her right brain, her intuitive knowledge. One is more apt to flow into an alpha state if in the energy field of another person in a relaxed alpha state, which is one of the reasons why fathers should also be familiar with the hypnosis tapes. (An *alpha state* is a state of peaceful relaxation characterized by alpha rhythms of the brainwaves, which can be recorded on an electroencephalograph machine, which graphs the brain impulses.)

Hypnosis is not dangerous to the uborn. In fact, quite the contrary is true. When a mother is stressed, adrenaline is released, thus allowing the catecholemines to cross the placental barrier, giving the uborn a stress cue. (*Catecholemines* are groups of chemicals made by the body that work as important nerve transmitters. They prepare the body to act based on flight-or-fight syndrome by elevating the blood pressure, increasing the heart rate, speeding the breathing, and shutting down digestion.) When a mother uses hypnotic techniques and is able to drift into a presleep state, she sends soothing messages across the placental barrier. By the sixth month, the cortex of the uborn's brain is able to take in messages and to retain them. It is advantageous to the mother to be relaxed and to send soothing messages to the uborn.

HOW TO BEGIN USING HYPNOSIS

It is advantageous to begin using the *Hypnosis and Pregnancy* tape early in your pregnancy. It helps you to prevent morning sickness and to remain in optimum health by beginning to address and relieve your fear and stress.

When you use hypnosis, you will first feel a visible release of tension, with slight involuntary movements of the extremities as they begin to relax. There is a deepening of the breath. After the muscles release, your breathing becomes slower, more regular, and shallow; your eyelids close, eye movements slacken, an occasional smile passes across your face, and tears can be released. You will feel an opening of your body and a relaxation of your jaw and your perineum. After sufficient practice, you can maintain the hypnotic condition with eyes opened in a state of somnambulism, walking about and following suggestions without affecting the trance state. This is important during the early stage of labor, when it is often more comfortable to be up and around.

ROLE OF THE FATHER
AND/OR SUPPORT PERSON

Many fathers respond to the woman's increased intimacy needs (not to be confused with sexual needs, which are often decreased during pregnancy) as an unnecessary demand and drain on their time and energy. This reaction invokes feelings of abandonment, fear, and helplessness in the mother, all of which are expressed to the uborn via placental circulation.

By educating fathers and partners on how to play an integral and important part in the birthing process, and by helping them to realize the importance of their participation, we establish a new expression of harmony toward the uborn. Now the joy of pregnancy, labor, and birthing can begin, for all are working together as a team. The father has connected to his positive mother instinct, nurturing himself and his wife in turn, and together they are nurturing their uborn.

Through the father's connection to his own nurturing self, he gets to experience a new kind of inner strength. The stress of pregnancy, instead of being a burden to the father and a period of isolation and loneliness for the mother, is transformed into a shared growth experience through which they each can learn an inner sense of balance.

In our classes, both fathers and mothers are hypnotized. Fathers can listen to the *Hypnosis for Labor* tape at least once to experience what it feels like to be hypnotized. This experience also helps fathers to get the cadence of the words right and to understand the process better. By being hypnotized, the fathers become better able to help the mothers into a hypnotic state. Fathers get a great sense of comfort from knowing that they can have such a profound and relaxing effect on their partner.

Often during the classes I teach on the Leclaire Method, fathers joke with each other: "I think I'll keep her in this state and have her wait on me hand and foot." Everyone laughs, but this is truly an important connection for the man. In some sense, he is looking for reassurance that his partner will still be nurturing to him when the baby arrives. Many mothers say that under usual circumstances, they would not feel comfortable abandoning themselves in this way to their partner. The pregnancy and imminent birth create a need in the woman to be taken care of, however, to be nurtured, to be intimate, and to be relaxed and free from pain. The need in the father is to be needed, to be competent, and to be able to expand his boundaries.

So hypnosis education can relieve both mother and father of the fear and tension surrounding childbirth. It allows the mother to enter into labor completely relaxed, calm, and serene in her knowledge that her body knows exactly how to birth her baby with a minimum of discomfort. At the same time, a mild hypnotic state puts the father as support person in an advantageous position. Through hypnosis, he is able to remain calm, competent, and energized. Through his participation in the classes during pregnancy and through his support during labor and birthing, he is able to contribute significantly to the quality of his partner's pregnancy, labor, and birthing process.

HOW HYPNOSIS WORKS

Hypnosis works through suggestions. Our minds are constantly given suggestive stimuli from both the external world and our own internal world. These suggestions have created both good and bad habits. In hypnosis, we attempt to replace the negative stimuli with positive. If we see the mind, the body, the spirit, and our emotions as a quartet, then we can perhaps see that harmony is necessary. If the spirit is peaceful, we can then have beautiful mental visions of a joyous birth, thus allowing pleasurable emotions. These pleasurable emotions help to maintain the neuromuscular harmony of the body. If the muscles of the body are relaxed, we are more readily able to avail ourselves of positive and relaxed mental images, and in turn, the relaxed mental images permit the association of pleasurable sensations and emotions. This serenity on a physical plane allows us to get in touch with the endless peace in our spirit.

There seems to be a correlation between emotions and muscle tension. Because the goal of hypnosis in childbirth is to decrease and to eliminate the discomforts of labor (when the mother and support person are willing), our first task is to eliminate tension in all involved peripheral parts and to relax all the muscle groups. When the body is relaxed, fear is an unwelcome visitor. Fear and relaxation are incongruent; the muscles of the uterus, used to expel the baby, are given little resistance from the relaxed body. Whether we start with the body, the mind, the spirit, or the emotions, relaxed and pleasant actions and images influence the fulfillment of a relaxed and joyous birth.

Breathing and Hypnosis

Hypnosis will keep you relaxed during labor. A relaxed body knows exactly how to breathe. A relaxed body always inhales and exhales properly, adapting totally to the situation at hand. Relaxing hypnotically helps you to stay in the moment, to stay with the self rather than to engage in the critical faculties of the ego—in the self outside of the now, the self that judges, discriminates, and labels. When you walk from the dark to the light, your pupils spontaneously shrink; you don't ask yourself how to make that happen. If you master the hypnotic techniques, your mouth will be relaxed, and your breathing will be spontaneously perfect.

You might want to practice relaxed breathing ahead of time. To begin, observe your breathing. Don't alter it in any way; just observe it. Next, place your hands on your lower abdomen. Inhale through your nose, and try to blow your abdomen up like a balloon. Fill it with air. Feel your hands rise. Now blow the breath out through your mouth with three slow breaths. Then relax your breathing and focus on it. Observe it once again, but don't alter it in any way.

Next, inhale a second time through your nostrils, filling your abdomen with air, feeling your hands rise with your abdomen, and again blowing the breath out through your mouth with three soft breaths. Relax your breathing. Observe it; don't alter it.

Now take another deep breath, filling your abdomen with air and blowing it out through your mouth softly and slowly. This time, pay particular attention to your exhalation, and breathe out completely, sending the breath out through your rectum and/or vagina. Repeat this inhalation and exhalation one more time.

During labor, you will automatically inhale through your nose, gently and deeply when necessary. You will feel as though you are exhaling through your vagina and/or your rectum.

Your Uterus During Hypnosis

The uterus has three muscle layers. All of these muscles need to work in harmony to allow for an easy and relaxed birth. One layer shortens and tightens, thus pushing the baby downward and out of the uterus. The second layer controls the blood supply, and the third, inner layer keeps the outlet open. The relaxation of the mother facilitates all this happening. If there is no cooperation, then the third layer acts in opposition to the first, and the outlet closes, thus inhibiting the progress of the baby through the birth canal. Now the muscles in opposition are experienced as tension. Tension causes pain, which allows fear to enter. Fear causes more tension and thus more pain, resulting in a further inhibition of progress. It is in this cycle that maternal and fetal distress can occur.

One of the main tasks of hypnosis is to prevent this undesirable cycle, for it is here that the tension manifests itself as a resistance to the birth. Any resistance to the birth is manifested by more tension, further inhibition of labor, and a tight cervix.

Hypnotic relaxation permits free circulation of the blood through the middle layer of the muscles, which in turn provides the necessary oxygen to the working muscles, which helps to keep the baby in a nonstressed, relaxed state during her journey out of the birth canal.

When a mother following the Leclaire Method experiences uterine contractions, she can relax her cervix, thus preventing the need for stronger uterine contractions. When she experiences deep pressure and stretching, she is able to relax into her pelvic floor. She is able to inhale through her nose or mouth and send the breath right through her cervix, out through her rectum or vagina in anticipation of the oncoming head.

Ankle Technique for Transition

During your most intense rhythmic risings, called *transition,* your support person will help distract you from any potential pain through a technique of squeezing your left ankle. This technique works because of the fact that the body is aware of only one sensation at a time. In an indigenous tribe in Africa, twelve-year-old boys are circumcised without natural or chemical anesthesia; they are given instead a thorn to press against the roof of their mouth and are told to focus there during the circumcision. They report that they are aware only of the roof of their mouths and not of the mutilation.

During transition, your support person will squeeze your left ankle. (Note: There is an acupressure point on the inner aspect of the leg above the ankle, about four fingers up, that helps to dilate the cervix—but practice the technique using this point only after week 39. Acupressure is an ancient Chinese healing art used to correct any imbalance in the flow of the vital forces in the body.) You will focus only on the hand squeezing your ankle. Because the left side of the body is controlled by the right side of the brain, squeezing here connects to the intuitive right brain. You will relax your jaw and your hands and send your breath out through your cervix and down your leg to your ankle.

This is a favorite technique of all who have tried it. It is simple, easy to do, and effective. When the contraction is over, the support person releases his or her hand and relaxes, while the mother rests silently until the next rhythmic rising or contraction. At that moment, you repeat the same routine.

You can demonstrate the effectiveness of this technique by having the support person squeeze both ankles of the mother hard while she is under hypnosis and having the mother focus only on her left ankle. She will be unaware of the right one. If this is done again when the mother is not under hypnosis, she will usually yell, "Ouch. I don't believe you really squeezed that hard before!"

Just remember: During transition, only squeeze one ankle—the left.

Hypnosis and Cesarean Sections

Despite their best efforts, a small percentage of women find themselves requiring a cesarean section even after preparing using the Leclaire Method. If this is the case for you, your hypnosis techniques will greatly help you to relax before surgery. Let your anesthesiologist know you are using hypnosis, as you may require less anesthesia. Mothers who have used the Leclaire Method throughout pregnancy and then need a cesarean section feel that the techniques greatly helped them to a rapid emotional and physical recovery postsurgery.

The Myth of Pain in Labor

We are virtually our own medicine cabinets, our own natural pharmacy with natural means of alleviating pain. No pain-killing drug will influence the body's perception of pain unless the body has a natural receptor site for this drug and is able naturally to produce the desired response to the drug. Artificial drugs that cover pain, in fact, are made to mimic the body's own reactions to pain. They create a substance that goes to a receptor site in the body and triggers a response from the body to relieve the pain. Artificial drugs are similar to natural "drugs," such as endorphins, so that they can bind to the same spot in place of the natural drug.

It has been observed that soldiers wounded in action need much less analgesic than do civilians with similar wounds. Why? Soldiers wounded in action looked forward to the benefits of removal from battle, safety, and returning home. War was no longer their daily experience. The war was over for the wounded soldier. For the civilian, injury meant loss of work and money, loss of the feeling of being safe in a usually safe environment. The civilian experienced fear, depression, and anxiety. These emotions tend to compound the experience of pain.

Pain is also created by association and by identification with a suggestive idea. In the example of the shark attack in Chapter Two, belief in a lifeguard's words, together with an individual's beliefs about sharks—not the shark itself—caused fear. If pain has become associated with a particular experience, you will expect it and thus experience it. This can happen even before the actual experience. If we dread something or expect it to hurt, it probably will.

Hypnosis is able to alleviate pain because it can influence the mother's psychological and emotional relation to childbirth, which plays an important role in the experience of contractions as painful rather than as gentle, rolling, amniotic waves moving you closer to birth. Our goal is to affect the body, thus affecting the activity of the mind, which in turn helps the body to release the desired beneficial secretions that promote balance and healing of pain and an increase in comfort and relaxation.

Most of us prejudge labor. It is not what we think it is. It is beyond the frontier of thought. The suffering of labor arises from within us. Breath by easy breath, we accept life. Contraction by contraction, we participate in and accept an easy or a painful birth. Just allow your contractions, and they will promote a feeling of relaxation, joy, and well-being, a mindfulness of one moment after another opening you to your birthing process.

A Note Regarding Contractions

Throughout the writings on and in your classes (and in this book), you have heard about "contractions." Because of the negative connotations associated with this word, it may be helpful to think of these movements of the uterus as "rhythmic risings." Your uterus is working to birth a baby, and you can call this work a *rush* or a *rising* or a *rhythmic rising*. Hypnobirthing techniques alter the way the brain perceives and interprets the intensity of the contractions, or rhythmic risings of the uterus, and activates the body's own comfort mechanism. If you say the words very slowly, the sound of the words themselves can help to synchro nize your mind with the work of your uterus. Saying the words "I'm having a rhythmic rising" can even make you smile or laugh. This creates a completely different atmosphere around your birth.

LABOR IN FULL AWARENESS

Beginning in week 39, play your *Hypnosis for Labor* tape (see Resources, or make your own tape from the following script) at least once each day. As soon as you go into the first stage of labor, rest and play your *Hypnosis and Pregnancy* tape. It will be familiar to you and give you an increased sense of comfort and trust in your own natural ability to birth your baby. Then go about your activities as you are able: walking, bathing, rocking in a chair, listening to music. Relax.

If you are birthing in a hospital, you should be there when your contractions are five minutes apart. Play your *Hypnosis for*

Labor tape with earphones on the way to the hospital so you don't hypnotize the driver. Or play your *Smart Beginnings Music* tape for all of you. Once you have arrived at the hospital and are settled, play your *Hypnosis for Labor* tape again, or have your support person read the following script to you. At this point, you should do only one thing at a time. You must remain completely mindful, living in the now.

HYPNOSIS FOR LABOR: A SCRIPT

Cover yourself with at least a light blanket, as you may feel chilly. Then go slowly through the following steps.

Step 1: *The easiest way to relax a muscle is to first exaggerate its contraction. The easiest way to relax your diaphragm is to focus on exhaling. Begin the relaxation by first getting in any comfortable position.*

Step 2: *The second step is to observe your breathing. Don't alter it in any way; just observe it. Now place one of your hands on your lower abdomen. Inhale through your nose. Try to blow your abdomen up like a balloon; fill it with air. Feel your hand rise. Now blow the breath out through your mouth with three slow, blowing-type breaths, then relax your breathing and focus on it. Again, observe your breathing, but don't alter it in any way.* (Often, when we breathe normally during waking hours, we don't have a great rise and fall of the abdomen; it is usually the chest and shoulders that rise.

In correct, relaxed breathing, the abdomen should rise and not the chest and shoulders. This deep breathing is different from our usual inhalation.) *Inhale a second time through your nostrils, filling the abdomen with air, feeling your hand rise with your abdomen, and again blowing the breath out through your mouth with three soft blowing breaths. Relax your breathing. Observe it; don't alter it in any way.*

Now take another deep breath, filling the abdomen with air, and blow it out through your mouth softly and slowly. This time, pay specific attention to your exhalation, breathe out completely, and send the breath out through your rectum and/or your vagina. Repeat this inhalation one more time.

Step 3: *Turn your focus toward your feet and ankles. Gently contract your feet and ankles; now contract them a bit more, and now relax them. Contract your calves, shins, and knees gently and then firmly, as tightly as you can, and now release them. Let go of all the tension in your lower legs.*

Turn your focus toward your thighs, buttocks, and genital area. Contract these areas gently, firmly, and now as tightly as you can. Relax your thighs; let go of all tension in your thighs, your buttocks, your genital area. Again, focus on your breathing. Don't alter it in any way; simply observe it.

Focus on your abdomen and all its contents. Become aware specifically of your uterus and your baby. Take a large, slow, deep abdominal breath and exhale it to your belly, to your uterus, to your baby, and out your rectum and/or your vagina. Let a deep sense of relaxation and peace float across your belly.

Now become aware of your spine. Begin to contract one vertebra at a time, and let the tension spread out from your spine across your back and up your sides until your entire back is arched with tension.

Feel the force of gravity pulling the tension out of your back and into the ground. Let go of all the tension in your back, and feel yourself sinking comfortably into the bed or chair.

Become aware now of your chest, your breasts. Contract them gently and relax them. Contract them again, gently, and then relax them again.

Now contract your neck, right and left, and front and back. Let go of the tension in your neck. Let it relax.

Begin to contract your shoulders, upper arms, elbows, lower arms, wrists, hands, fingers. Make fists with your hands. Now extend your arms and spread your fingers as wide apart as you can.

Relax your shoulders, arms, and hands. Take a deep breath, and send the breath down your spine. Take another deep abdominal breath, and send it down your arms. Feel yourself letting go of all tension in your body.

Now we come to the head and face, the most important part of relaxation. Many of us hold tension in our jaws. Clench your jaw for a moment, and observe the tension beginning to return to the rest of your body. Now relax your jaw, and let your mouth fall open. Turn your attention toward your scalp, your hair follicles, your forehead, your eyebrows, your eyelids, the area around your eyes, your temples, your cheekbones, your jaw, your chin, your ears, your nose, your nostrils, your lips, your tongue, your gums and teeth, the mucous membrane lining of your mouth, your throat. Now swallow, and scrinch your entire face up like a prune; harder now, tighter, clench your jaw. Now let it all go. Relax your face; feel the weight and the heaviness in your eyelids. Let them remain comfortably closed.

Now, with your mouth slightly open, begin to scan your body with your mind's eye to locate any areas of your body that are still tense. Now contract those areas of your body that are still tense, and slowly relax them. Take a deep abdominal breath, and send the breath to those areas and then out through your rectum and/or your vagina.

Step 4: *Once again, just focus on your breathing, not alter-ing it, just observing it. Now begin to visualize a staircase of ten steps. You may design them any way you want. You may place them anywhere you want. Some women like to climb down into a comfortably safe and shallow pool of water, where they can float; a place where, if possible, it might be comfortable to birth their baby.*

Now begin to climb down the staircase, counting to yourself and having your support person count you down.

10. Down.

9. And deeper, deeper, and down.

8. Deeper, now, down deeper.

7. Your arms and legs feel totally relaxed.

6. Deeper and deeper and down; all sounds other than your support person's voice are out of your awareness; if any other sounds enter your consciousness, they will only serve to deepen your state of relaxation, peace, and serenity.

5. Deeper now, down deeper.

4. *Your face and jaw are totally relaxed.*

3. *Deeper and deeper and down.*

2. *Your eyelids are very, very heavy; you could open them if you wanted to, but you don't really want to open them.*

1. *Feeling totally comfortable and centered, better than you have felt in a long, long time.*

Step 5: *Now turn your attention to the area between your two eyebrows and, with your eyes closed, look into this area, also known as your third eye.*

(The support person can now be quiet for a minute while the mother begins to center herself and relax herself even more deeply through focusing into her third eye. Then the support person continues to read.)

The work and practice of looking into the third eye are most important, as it is the place of deepest relaxation. It is within this point that you are to focus while you are pushing. If you can relax during the contractions of the first stage of labor, and if you can relax in between the contractions during the second stage, and if you can look deeply into your third eye, relaxing your jaw, keeping your eyes closed, and pushing from deep in your third eye, your circular muscles will be loose and relaxed, and childbirth will progress normally and naturally.

You will have a great sense of your labor paying off; you will have a great sense of accomplishment. Through your third eye, you get in touch with your body's perfect knowledge of how to birth your baby. Your body knows exactly what to do, how to push, when to push, how to breathe, when to inhale, when to exhale. All you have to do is practice, practice, practice, and trust your body's intuition and stay relaxed. Once you have engaged the critical faculties of your mind, you are no longer experiencing the moment; you are no longer trusting your body's perfect knowledge. All you have to do is tell yourself, "I am relaxing. I am focusing on my third eye. It is beneficial for me to believe, to know that I can birth my baby in a comfortable and relaxed manner. I am willing to work hard to push when I need to do so; I will lose myself in my work. I am relaxed now. I am more deeply relaxed than I've been in a long, long time."

Now begin to project way out into the universe a big ball of crimson red light. As you look at the light, it comes closer and closer and closer until it fades away, leaving you looking once again into your third eye.

Now project way out into the universe a big ball of violet light. It, too, begins to come closer and closer and closer

*until it fades away; again you are looking into your third
eye, this time more deeply than before.*

*Now project way out into the universe a big ball of emerald
green light, and as it gently bounces toward you, it fades
away. This time you are looking more deeply, more peacefully into your third eye.*

*Deeper and deeper into your third eye, you relax deeply into
it. Now project way out into the universe a big ball of orange
light. Closer and closer it comes to you until it fades, and
now you are peacefully, blissfully back into the serenity of
your third eye. You are becoming more and more familiar
with the omniscience in you.*

*You enjoy the depth and the peace. Now you project way out
into the universe a big ball of yellow light. It is splendid out
there. It comes in closer and closer, and gently fades away.
You are deeply centered, and you look into your third eye. A
great sense of peace and comfort and courage fills your being.*

*Now you project way out into the universe a big ball of blue
light. This ball of light is different from the others. As it
comes close to you, it bursts into a magnificent, warm, healing white light, much like the healing, soothing rays of the
sun. The white light begins to surround you, envelop you,
and soothe you even more. You feel caressed by it. It begins*

to flow down through the top of your skull, down through the medulla oblongata, down your spine to the base of your spine, and when it reaches the base of your spine, the healing white light begins to radiate throughout all of your extremities. It flows down through your right hip, and leg, and foot, and toes, and through your left hip, leg, foot, and toes. It flows down through your shoulders, into your arms, through your wrists, and into your hands and fingertips. The white healing light now begins to fill your chest cavity and fill your heart with a warmth and a love and an acceptance of yourself that you haven't felt in a long time.

The healing white light flows out of your heart into your abdomen. It surrounds your uterus and penetrates your uterus and lines the walls of your uterus with a healing white light. The light surrounds your baby and places your baby in the proper birthing position. It helps your baby to grow normally, naturally, comfortably, and healthily. It relaxes the baby and tells the baby that you are a calm, loving, and nurturing mother. You will be able to use the white light as an ally during pregnancy, labor, birthing, and postpartum.

In this state of deep relaxation, make a circle on your chest with the middle finger of your left hand. This is called an anchor. As you make this anchor, remind yourself with the following statements: "I will visualize the white light present within. It is my ally. I am filled with peace, hope, and com-

fort. I am again relaxed and able to go with the flow of my
body. I am again able to celebrate the birthing of my baby."

(This is your anchor. Every time you make this circle, you
will immediately be in a deep, concentrated state of focus.
The more you make this circle, the deeper you will go into
relaxation. When you are in a deep state of relaxation, peace,
and serenity, you may drop your hand to a place where it is
comfortable. This anchor is your ability to instantly put
yourself into a deep hypnotic trance. It will work for you
whenever you want it to, especially during labor, transition,
and birth. You would never use this technique while driving
a moving vehicle.

Repeat this technique any time you or your support person
feel that you are no longer in an alpha state. Always remember to allow your exhalations to be complete, breathing
through the contractions and out through your rectum
and/or your vagina. It is a good idea to practice this anchor
technique throughout your pregnancy. It works like a
charm.)

Now I am going to clap my hands, and you will be wide
awake. (Clap.) *Now make the circle on your chest with the*
middle finger of your left hand as many times as you need to
in order to automatically put yourself into a deep healing
hypnotic trance and relax your hand when you are in it.

(The support person is silent and waits for the mother to drop her hand. Both are quiet for a minute or five, enjoying the peace and serenity. Then the support person continues. If this hypnosis is being done before bedtime or during labor, you would give the suggestion, *Now you will fall into a deep, peaceful, natural sleep, only to awaken when you need to, feeling refreshed and relaxed and fully awake.* Otherwise, the support person will count up the mother, saying the following.)

I am now going to count you up from one to five. When we reach five, you will be wide awake and refreshed and relaxed and confident that you can calmly and comfortably birth your baby at term in an easy vaginal passage. (Support person slowly counts up mother from one to five.)

1. *Begin to stretch your arms and your legs.* (Support person should be silent for at least thirty seconds.)

2. *Take a deep awakening breath.* (Support person should be silent for at least thirty seconds.)

3. *Slowly become aware of the sounds around you.* (Support person should be silent for at least thirty seconds.)

4. *Your eyelids are no longer heavy.* (Support person should be silent for at least thirty seconds.)

5. *Your eyes are wide open; you are awake and refreshed and relaxed, and you will be aware and wide awake enough to drive safely and legally, whenever you need to do so.*

A Word About Transition

Mindfulness is being in the now, just being in the middle of labor in the eye of the now. Our definition of transition is the time in labor when you are not having inner dialogue; you are not anticipating anything; you are in the moment. You have no ego, no awareness of yourself. You are in the navel, the umbilicus, the deep center of the omnipresent. *Now.*

All the practice that you have practiced, all the work that you have worked, all the preoccupation with what labor is like, all your fears and all your unfelt feelings that would come out during transition have dissipated because you have given reverence to them during your pregnancy. All your preparation has paid off.

Transition now can become a time when you cling to nothing and reject nothing. You have no anticipation of what the state of transition is like. Your practice has paid off. You are in a state of equanimity, no longer preoccupied, totally present. Transition becomes a time of the now, a gift of being in freedom and acceptance—nonexpectations, nonthoughts, just a distillation of all that is and a clarity of the moment. You do not know this is labor; you do not know this is transition; you do not know you are dilating; you do not know you are close to giving birth. You know nothing. You just are.

You are in a state of amazing freedom, a state of liberation from suffering from pain. A state of being. Perhaps the fear of being in the moment is that you have let go of all else, like the infant who doesn't see his mother or his ball and knows they have disappeared. "If I don't keep all my loved ones in my mind, they may disappear, and I shall never be able to get them back, or they will know I have abandoned them, and they could suffer." Someone has to suffer. It is I, or it is they. What an untenable choice. I choose therefore to live in the past or in the future. It is safer that way. When we are truly in the moment, however, nothing is missing.

The only way to transcend any potential pain of childbirth is to be willing to feel every sensation of the process, just as you did in your pregnancy meditations. During transition, you may want to use your anchor to deepen your state of hypnosis. Hypnosis also helps you to forget about time. Being completely in the moment, without worrying about what is to come or what has passed, is the benefit of being in a hypnotic state.

Chapter Four

AVOIDING THE EMOTIONAL ROLLER COASTER

The Effects of Meditation and Imagery

Prior to conception, you should make a point to acknowledge that you are preparing the uterine nursery for your uborn. That preparation is discussed extensively in *Twelve Weeks to Fertility*. (See Resources section for more information.) Once you have conceived, you must establish and maintain the connection between you and your uborn. She is alive and present in you. Be still, and you will know she is present. Be still. Be!

What your uborn needs are peace and safety, calm and serenity, beautiful music, loving care, healing voices, nourishing maternal emotions, and a healthy body to pouch about in.

I am not discussing—nor am I advocating—prenatal stimulation and education. In fact, I think they are dangerous. Trying to educate our children before birth is too much too soon. In my experience, babies will learn best and be brightest if they are allowed to follow their own learning rhythms. This is especially true before birth. Uborns do *not* need to be taught anything. They are truly perfect exactly the way they are. They do need to be acknowledged, comforted, listened to, or felt. (Their movements are messages to Mommy.)

The communications of uborns need to be addressed. Uborns can become frantic when they hear rock music or yelling from either parent. Pay attention to these movements and silent messages and alter your environment to suit your forty-week gestation. Rubbing or patting your belly in response to or in initiation to your uborn is okay. Play our specially designed music tape, *Leclaire Smart Beginnings Music*, or a tape of Gregorian chants or Baroque music for your uborn's developing awareness of sound. Speak in loving ways, not for the purpose of educating, teaching, or stimulating, but for the purpose of connecting and acknowledging that you are at one with each other. After all, your uborn is another organ of your body during gestation. One of the most important aspects of your relationship to your uborn is respect. If you decide to communicate, and your uborn doesn't feel responsive, you know his regular movements, and you know that he is healthy; you need to respect his desire to rest and not to respond to your need for communication.

During a hypnosis session, we frequently notice that uborns respond to the lack of motion by tumbling about. When the uborn's mother or father (or I) explains to him what we are doing and that this is a rest time and why we are resting, he calms down. It's amazing. It reminds me of a day I spent recently on the beach in Malibu. I was walking with a friend south along the beach, and a school of porpoises swam by, about thirty yards offshore, going north. We did an about-face and decided to see if we could communicate with the sea animals. We talked to them as we walked. We said we were turning around and going the other way. Come with us. We did, and they did. We were like children—gleeful and incredulous. We did it again, and they did, too. We skipped along the water's edge and played. We were as one. The third time we did it, they kept going "their" way. We said good-bye and thanked them for the game as they continued north and we south.

It is important to communicate with your uborn but not to stimulate her. *Overstimulated minds become overwhelmed, and overstimulated bodies can become ill.* I have been working with mothers-to-be using the Leclaire Method for many years. In fact, one of the first children born to one of these mothers is now fourteen. The babies born through this program develop well and seem to have a zest for life. They are curious and aware. They are usually treated with respect, as both mother and father learn that long before the baby is born. The race and registration for the best nursery school do not deeply affect Leclaire moms and dads. They realize that their child knows exactly how to grow and develop with the proper attention, nourishment, care, love, and respect. The most important gifts that you can give your child during gestation and the first year of life are your attention, your care, your understanding, your listening, your loving gaze, your milk, your frequent presence.

One mother (a lawyer) told me that she was just too busy to play her music tape or to play her hypnosis tape or to meditate.

"I'll wait till he arrives," she said.

"He has," I answered. "He can hear and feel and experience your way of being. He arrives at implantation. Don't go worrying about his nanny or his nursery school or his education. You are his nanny. You are his nursery, and you are his education. All that you do for your uborn is more important than all you can do for him for the rest of his life. How exciting that we can play an active part in the growth and development of our uborns."

In this chapter, you will learn how to avoid the emotional roller coaster that occurs when you fail to address and become aware of your limitations, fears, hopes, wishes, and anxieties. To address your emotions, you need to sit still long enough to be aware of them. This chapter gives background and methods for two techniques that will allow you to do this: meditation and imagery. By calming your own self, you can change the world: You can bring peace and respect and serenity and understanding to the world one baby at a time.

MEDITATION AND HOW IT CAN
AFFECT YOUR PREGNANCY

Many of us act like a bundle of energy constantly in motion. We cannot stop. We go and go and go and go and obsess and control and create and clean and pray and play and dream and shop and read and write and jog and go on the "life cycle" and drive our new SUVs and become enraged at stop signs and crosswalks and play music and dance and learn new languages and boogie board and see every new film and play and watch every sport known to man and flip from one station to another and talk on the phone and go to therapy or analysis and make love and have our nails done and our faces lifted and our kitchens redone and travel and observe other cultures. All of these things are ways of trying to fill our lives. Filling the minutes and hours and days of our lives is our effort to allay our anxiety and to make extinct our seemingly endless cravings. We are insatiable, as everyone knows. We are the infants of infinity craving its bliss.

There is, however, a way of being still that can truly be an aid to pregnancy, labor, birth, postpartum, and all of life. It's a form of stillness that I hesitate to mention so early in the book for fear of losing you: It's called meditation. Many people believe that meditation is tied to some form of religious practice, and perhaps that form of religion isn't compatible with their own beliefs. I describe meditation as a form of stillness that allows each person's own mind and body to come to rest, allowing for rejuvenation. By using meditation as a way to find stillness and calm, many women find that during labor they can go to that calm state easily. Because meditation is so helpful, I hope you will try it right away. Let's begin by trying to understand the process of meditation. We'll explore the form, the practice, and the purpose of meditation for your pregnancy and labor.

Many people buy books and books and more books on meditation and take various meditation classes only to debunk meditation as not working. It didn't work for these people for one simple reason: They never practiced it. I know a young mother who is infatuated with meditation, for example, but refuses to practice it on a daily or even a weekly basis. She believes she does not have time to do it for herself, but meditation only works when you do it for yourself. It is not like a massage, or an epidural, or a pedicure. She can't have it done to her or for her.

A Natural State

I intuitively learned how to meditate as a child and made use of this skill often because my father suffered from traumatic war neuroses. I found meditation most healing. I stopped meditating for many years after I had children; I didn't think I had time to meditate. However, when I stopped smoking, meditation became my substitute for cigarettes, and I have now decided it is something I shall never stop doing again in my life. The benefits certainly outweigh what I have thought of as interruptions or inconveniences. Now I look at meditation as a fantastic respite, a renewal of mental, physical, and spiritual energy. It is an amazing gift and a wonderful place that I can go. Meditation also brings us more into contact with our inner knowing, what many call "intuition." This knowing is not something odd or spooky. It is nothing more than understanding without a conscious thinking. My *Oxford Dictionary* defines it as "immediate apprehension by the mind without reasoning; immediate apprehension by a sense; immediate insight." Perhaps it is only our instinct being allowed to surface above the "noise" we make in our own minds.

Meditation is simply a quieting of the mind, with no attachment to the outcome. There are different ways of meditating.

What I have chosen to explain here is specifically to prepare you for the meditation of labor and birth. *I thought I was going to be learning hypnobirthing, not meditation birthing*, you say? You've been duped—or are you learning both, and what is the difference? First, let's look at what hypnobirthing and hypnosis are and what they are not.

Hypnobirthing is done to you from the outside, with your participation and your active permission. You listen to a tape or to someone saying the hypnotic suggestions aloud to you, or you say the hypnotic procedure aloud or silently to yourself. Even if you are not saying the words, you are following the words to be led into a state of relaxation in which you let go of certain thoughts. In meditation, you simply observe. You do not have a script for yourself, nor do you systematically contract and release your muscle groups as you do in hypnosis.

But what *can* you do through meditation? As you know, we experience life through our five senses—sight, sound, touch, taste, and smell—and through our sixth sense, our thought. In order to be still and to be present in the now—not aware of the past, not trying to be aware of the future, but just aware of the present—it is helpful to observe the processes of our senses.

To me, the most crucial aspect of meditation, especially for mothers-to-be, is the quieting of body and mind and the letting go of the outcome, even though the result is often an approach of the absolute and a healing of mind, body, and spirit. It is also a letting go of our long search for satisfaction and an entering into the light beyond the mind.

Not an Antireligious Activity

People who practice some Christian religions believe that meditation goes against their religion, that meditation is a religion in and of itself, or that it is a New Age fad. Those who believe in God and who practice religions that do not promote meditation or are even against it, however, might keep in mind that a sincere meditation practice can improve your conscious contact with the infinite. How can that go against your religion?

Those who do not believe in God and who believe that meditation is a form of a religion or a theist practice of some sort should remember that meditation brings you in touch with your own peace and freedom and can improve your conscious contact with the grandeur of the infinite blackness. This to me sounds like a connection to the omnipresent now and a deep stillness. Perhaps some of the goals are the same as those of religion, but meditation itself is certainly not a dogma or a religion.

Different practitioners define meditation in different ways. Some consider it a way to solve problems, the simple act of focusing attention on a puzzle or concern. Others see it as a ritual of contemplation, something "practiced" in a structured way, perhaps with guidance, music, or special incense or pillows. Still others see it as a way to help guide their lives toward a particular goal. Meditation is all of these things, in fact, and it can be as structured or as unstructured as you prefer.

The Benefits of Meditation for Mothers-to-Be

Meditation will avail you of your conscious contact with your unconscious. When you allow your feelings to emerge in this state and allow yourself to become of them and to feel them, you begin to understand their origin. Anything that you want to change must first begin with awareness and an understanding. The more you do this exercise, the more you are able to be in the now. Even if the only benefit you receive is that you have rested for twenty minutes, that is sufficient.

The entire program of the Leclaire Method and hypnosis is about doing all the work and the practices without being attached to the outcome. Allow the entire process of working this book to be a meditation. That means to be mindful, to be present for yourself and your uborn when you are reading and doing the work in this book. Do not let yourself be preoccupied.

To be totally in the moment—while dressing, when opening and closing a door, when walking, when listening—is to live mindfully. As an example of an individual who lives mindfully, I recall a Vietnamese physician who was doing immunological research at the University of Southern California and whom we invited to join us for dinner so that we could discuss mind/body medicine when I worked at the Simonton Cancer Center. We were excited about his coming and couldn't wait to dine with him. After he arrived, we had a lovely dinner, but it was silent. This doctor does not speak while he eats. He enjoys his food mindfully, one bite at a time. He explained to us later that he believes we could heal most diseases if we lived our entire lives mindfully.

It is most difficult for the Western-trained mind to understand this. I swim outside daily, for example, and when I remember, I try to swim mindfully. It is actually incredibly beautiful to watch your hands and arms cut the water, to watch the white bubbles rise as your fingers glide through the blue, to see the dappled light on the bottom. I succeed for two laps, though, and then drift and plan and think before bringing myself back to mindfulness.

In meditation, you "stand back" from your own will and allow all the good that is in you to come forward. That does not mean that all of your dark side won't surface. It will, but the continuity of meditation will skim it off the top as it arises, and eventually you will be left with the sweetness and goodness and loving kindness that are within—to the essentiality of your creation. Through meditation, you learn to be who you are rather than doing, doing to prove who you are or who you want to be.

In our world of business, we want to know what the outcome of our productivity is. If I do this, what will follow? This is like asking the question, Why should I continue to breathe? Breath is the life of your body. Meditation is the breath of your spirit. With it, you can live fully. With it, you are available to all that there is. It can be called infinite wisdom, infinite possibility, higher power, God, or the absolute. Whatever you choose to call it, meditation is the pilgrimage; meditation is your enjoyment with the boundless. The purpose of meditation is not to get profound insights or visions. We are merely trying to be still, to accept all of whom we are and let go of self-reflection as the center of the universe. Through meditation, we paradoxically come to know, however, beyond the intellect, the infinite, the absolute, the grand silence.

EXERCISE: LEARNING TO MEDITATE

If you follow these simple steps for the next few weeks, you will find yourself falling into your own habits of letting go and relaxing or, if you prefer, meditating. That's really all meditation is: sitting and letting your mind/body balance.

WEEK 1: To begin meditation, sit in a chair with your spine straight and feet flat on the floor, hands resting in your lap. You may also lie on your side with a pillow to help support your body, your belly, or anything else that needs to be supported. Turn the telephone off.

Settle yourself in your position, or just sit or lie for one to two minutes before you begin. The purpose of meditation is to still your mind. An easy way to do this is to focus your attention on some point in front of you or above you and then to concentrate on this focal point. If you are like most people, thoughts will continually enter your consciousness. No problem. Just observe the thoughts as you would a balloon floating up into the sky. Do not try to push the thoughts away, and don't try to hold on to them. Just continue to observe them without judgment. Do this for about five minutes, three times the first week.

WEEK 2: Practice in this new way three times this week. Begin as in week 1. Continue to maintain your state of one-pointedness while observing any thoughts that may enter. Along with your thoughts, you may now become aware of any feelings that emerge. Often people are afraid to sit still because some feelings they have been running from for ages come into awareness. This is possible. The great thing about this is that, if you allow yourself to feel the feelings for a few minutes, way into the depths of them, rather than ignore them, they will diminish in intensity and begin to ripple away. A newfound peace will be in their place. That is not to say that if you feel the feelings they will never return. It does mean, however, that we are always in a state of change and that, rather than running from what we might be afraid to feel (which in itself is exhausting, unsettling, debilitating, and immune suppressing), it is easier to face the feelings whenever they emerge, thus reaping the repeated benefit of the ensuing peace. There are ever-greater possibilities in this process: the hope of utter silence within, bliss, a deepening sense of oneness with the universe, and a feeling of boundless delight. A new dimension of the self can present a reality more comfortable and peaceful than any on this plane. It is a chance to dance into the infinite with the absolute. Once our fears surface, we can deal with them; in many cases, they go away altogether. Fears come and go as the undulations of your belly in labor, as the rhythmic risings of your uterus.

WEEK 3: Continue the same as in weeks 1 and 2. This week, begin to observe your breath. You don't need to alter your breathing in any way. Just observe your inhalation and your exhalation. Let this observation take precedence over the observation of your thoughts. Your thoughts may persist, but focus your attention on your breath.

In this observation of your breath, all else recedes. The breath, the now, the simplicity of the moment become effortless. Continue this focus for a few minutes, five times this week.

WEEK 4: Earlier I said that the purpose of meditation is to still the mind. That can create another longing, however, another kind of pain. So for now, let's look at the purpose of meditation as just to do it: just to meditate. Close your eyes and focus on the area between your eyebrows (also known as "the third eye"). Do this for five minutes four times a week.

WEEK 5: Continue as with weeks 1 through 4. Let these steps take you about five minutes. Use your own internal clock. Today and four more times this week, meditate for a total of twenty minutes each time. Conventional medicine has rendered you powerless. Our society is stuck. We have given the responsibility for our healing to our tribal doctors. That is because we respect them and have lost respect for ourselves. What aspects and details of your innate qualities do you not pay attention to? Take the time now to give consideration to your own intuitions. Remember past lies; allow present lies to come to the fore. You have the ability to use the energy of the authentic healer in you, this is your true medicine.

EXERCISE: A SIMPLE MEDITATION FOR QUIETING YOUR SENSES AND MIND

Read this through once, and then go back and try it. Then decide how often you would like to practice this for the greatest benefit. If you are in your first or second trimester, I suggest doing the following for five minutes three times each week and gradually working up to the goal of twenty minutes five times per week. That may take you six weeks or more. If you are in your third trimester, I suggest starting this practice for twenty minutes once a week and working your way up to the goal of twenty minutes five times a week.

You are now ready to meditate for twenty minutes at a sitting five times per week. It is a good idea to sit in a comfortable chair with your back as straight as is comfortable for you. You may elevate your legs on an ottoman if this is better for you.

Now let us begin. This is your Leclaire Method meditation:

1. *Eyes:* Become aware of your eyes, and become aware of what you see with your eyes. Become aware of the shadows, the light, the darkness, the colors, the shapes, the space, the objects. This awareness of what you see may bring up feelings. Feel the feelings, whatever they are. Gently close your eyes and move inward, into yourself.

2. *Ears:* Become aware of your ears. Listen to all the sounds around you and in the distance. Become fully aware of them. Feel whatever feelings may arise and move into your inner self.

3. *Mouth:* Become aware of your mouth, your lips, your tongue, the mucous membrane lining of your mouth, your saliva. Become aware of the taste in your mouth. Feel any feeling that may arise and move in you.

4. *Skin:* Become aware of your skin. Experience all that is touching you: the textures, the pressure. Again feel any feelings that may arise and move in you.

5. *Nose:* Become conscious of your nose and your nostrils. Become aware of any scents or fragrances, any smells. Feel the air as you inhale through your nostrils. Feel the feelings that may arise. Allow yourself to respond to the feelings, laughter, tears, a smile, a frown, a deep feeling. Experience what you are feeling. Don't push the feelings away; just allow them. They will pass. Everything does. Everything changes.

6. *Mind:* Now become aware of your mind, your thoughts. Observe your thoughts, the objects of your mind. Let them come, and then let them go and let yourself feel the feeling that your thoughts may evoke.

7. *Body:* Now become aware of your body. Go wherever it takes you. Just follow it. Do this for about ten breaths (one breath equals one inhalation and one exhalation). Now deliberately turn your attention to your uterus and your uborn. Put your hands on your abdomen and just be with your uterus and your uborn. Be with yourself; be with your uborn. Be still. Be.

You are probably beginning to feel a stillness, a quiet, a relaxation. The object is to be in the moment, to feel all that arises, which paves the way for a quieting of the mind. Now focus on your breath. Don't alter your breath in any way; just observe it. I'm breathing in. I'm breathing slowly out. In and out and in and out. Just rest and observe your breath.

Breathing and Meditation

The purpose of observing your breath is to keep you in the now. Your body knows exactly how to breathe, even during labor. All you need to do is be mindful of your breath. Observe it and observe it and continue to observe it. Continue to receive the next breath. Your jaw will relax. Your hands will relax. This practice of observing your breath will benefit your labor when you reach it. Using the breath to calm yourself will seem like second nature by then, and you and your support person can use it to remain calm and focused.

This is all you need to do when you meditate. Many feelings will arise when you begin to focus on your breath. It's okay. Feel them. They, too, will pass. Continue to focus on your breath.

EXERCISE: SETTING GOALS

Begin by doing the simple meditation described in the previous exercise once a week, and increase gradually until you are meditating six days a week for twenty minutes a day. Write out a schedule for yourself. Make the goals easier to meet than not to meet. Do not set yourself up for failure. We human beings change slowly. Respect who you are. Make your goals measurable and doable.

Here is a sample goal chart. (See Appendix, page 231, for a blank chart for readers to use.)

My Meditation Goals

Week 1: I will meditate Saturday at 4 P.M. for five minutes. I'll turn phone off.

Week 2: I will meditate Saturday and Sunday at 4 P.M. for ten minutes. I'll turn phone off.

Week 3: Same as week 2.

Week 4: I will meditate Wednesday before dinner for twenty minutes; Saturday and Sunday at 4 P.M. for twenty minutes. I'll turn phone off.

Week 5: Same as week 4.

Week 6: Same as week 5.

Week 7: I will meditate Monday before dinner, Wednesday before dinner, Saturday and Sunday at 4 P.M. for twenty minutes. I'll turn phone off.

Week 8: Same as week 7.

Week 9: Same as week 8.

IMAGERY AND HOW IT CAN AFFECT YOUR PREGNANCY

While meditation may be defined as emptying the mind to make space for our inner self to speak to us, or clearing the mind of clutter, there are other ways to use the power of our minds. One way is through imagery. Imagery could be defined as a formalized approach to daydreaming; we've all used it, whether we are aware of it or not. Have you ever found yourself smiling as you think of a pleasant time you have had, for example? Have you had a very clear vision of the way you would decorate the baby's room if money were no object? Both of these are forms of imagery. In the Leclaire Method, I have used imagery to help many women sort through and come to terms with negative thoughts or emotions about pregnancy, labor, birth, and motherhood.

As you learned in Chapter Two, emotions and thoughts can have a profound effect on our bodies. Our emotions affect the flow of our blood, constricting or dilating our blood vessels. Likewise, our bodies can limit the expansion of our minds. Even if our minds want us to, we can't necessarily "leap tall buildings in a single bound" or fly through the air, for example. If our bodies say stop, we can't continue reading or working on mental challenges endlessly. We can't memorize the encyclopedia. If our mind goes in one direction, then, will our body follow? If our mind does not want pain, how can we create that reality?

The goal is to become conscious of our behavior and thus to direct change and redirect our biological responses. I have observed that our unconscious reactions to our experiences are "habits." It is necessary to redirect these habits at a time when we are not stuck in a situation, at a time when we are relaxed and are not pushed to alter our behavior at that very moment. The purpose of trying to change unhealthy mind/body responses during pregnancy is to allow for the free flow of blood supply to the brain and uterus and uborn.

Using imagery is one good way to do this. It seems that imagery can be used to train the autonomic nervous system so that its two branches do not act as antagonists. The first of these branches, the sympathetic nervous system, regulates the function of the body as a result of unconscious thoughts or involuntary or habitual reactions; it enables us to mobilize in reaction to emergency situations, creating the fight-or-flight syndrome we all have heard about. This system allows us to use our adrenaline instead of letting our adrenaline use us. It mobilizes our neurotransmitters in a true emergency situation.

Our goal is to reverse the negative training we have received to respond to certain situations that do *not* warrant a fight-or-flight response and to help our body return to its natural intelligence. This is where the other branch of our autonomic nervous system—the parasympathetic system—comes in. This is the branch that slows our heartbeat, that enables us to respond rather than to react, that allows us to relax. The idea is not to live according to whatever training we might have received that is biologically destructive to us. Our goal is to create a space between the two branches of the nervous system where a new choice can be offered. It is really nerve reeducation.

Recently I discussed the mind/body connection with a friend, who told me how she had dealt with the trauma she felt surrounding her relationship with her father. She had decided in her early twenties that instead of consciously dealing with her feelings for her father, she would find a safe transition object for herself. She chose the actor Walter Pidgeon, because he was handsome, was dignified, and had a soothing, caring voice. He was a father she could live with. So she began to imagine him as her father.

My friend is a practicing analyst and said that most of the traditional diehards don't believe in lightening the burden. For her, it was the simplest thing to do, however. Her relationship with her father was so intolerable that she needed something more pleasant to look at in her mind's eye. Her mind wasn't fooled, but her body was. "If someone had asked me, 'Is Walter Pidgeon your father?' I wouldn't have said yes." She laughed.

It wasn't a delusion; it was more of an agreement for the moment, to give herself a break. To find relief, she agreed to lighten up, to have a delightful father. During the time when she was using imagery to "create" a father figure for herself, she was walking down the street one day when a very handsome, dignified man flirted and asked her out for a drink. She laughed again and said, "Be careful what you think." The man who approached her was very similar in manner to the "father" she had created in her imagination. She believes that this fantasy father, this transitional object, allowed her to later marry and have a wonderful and healthy relationship with her husband.

This is a good example of imagery. My friend allowed her mind to become the good mother of her body. She created a relief system like endorphins. She didn't have to pretend that she was strong and cared for by her new father for hours on end. She just did it for a few minutes at a time. It was time limited, like the intensity of a contraction.

Imagery can mean the difference between an exhausted, traumatized body and a relaxed, comforted body. Imagery is an important part of the preparation for childbirth.

One of the best ways to develop positive imagery for your pregnancy is to draw a picture of yourself, your partner, and your uborn, as you did in Chapter Two.

Case Study: Barbara

One day I was making a hospital visit to a mother, Barbara, who was on bed rest for preterm labor. She did not want to talk about having a baby for fear of something happening. She jokingly referred to her uterine passenger as "the lump" so as to distance herself from her feelings for her uborn.

"We don't have to discuss your birthing of your baby now, but it would be helpful if you could acknowledge that you already have a baby; you just can't see him yet."

"Oh, okay, I guess I do."

"Can you call him something other than 'the lump'?"

"Yes," she agreed. "I can call him Baby Smith."

That was a step closer to acknowledging a life growing inside her.

"Is it all right with you if I put my hands on your abdomen and talk with him?" I asked her.

"Oh, yes, please do. Sit on the bed and do it. I feel self-conscious, so I can't do it, but it's okay if you do it."

Her face looked excited and shy at the same time. Someone was going to acknowledge her child, something she appeared to want to do but was unable to do.

I started telling the uborn about his mother. "I am sitting here on the bed in the hospital with your mommy. She's smiling at you now. She's been taking good care of you, eating healthy, exercising gently. She wants you very much, but she's afraid to talk with you because it seems silly and it might make her feel closer to you. It's not that she doesn't want to feel close to you. It's just that if she really bonds and something happens to you she would be so devastated. She's afraid she couldn't deal with it."

Barbara kept smiling at me periodically, shyly, as if to say, "Go ahead, I like this." I continued speaking: "As of this moment, you seem pretty healthy. One thing that your mother and I have discussed is her trying to separate her anxiety from her deep inner knowing. Right now, your mommy is calm, and when I asked her how she thinks you are doing, she said she knew that you were healthy."

We went on in this vein for about fifteen minutes. Then Baby Smith's mother took a turn, putting her hands on her own belly and silently speaking to her uborn, connecting with thoughts and images. She felt good doing this and was proud of her progress. When the nurse came in to check her monitor, she noted that Barbara's uterus had quieted down significantly.

Chapter Five

HEALTHY MOTHER, HEALTHY BABY

Your Pregnancy Health Plan

Much of the work you have done so far has been mental work, preparing your mind for the changes to come. This book is about the mind/body connection and the growth and health of mother and baby, however, not just about the mind. Care for your physical needs is just as important as your mental care. Pregnancy is a good time to create healthy eating and exercise habits—habits that can work toward a healthy life even after your baby is born.

HEALTHY FOOD TO BUILD HEALTHY BABIES

Everything that you take in can contribute to the nourishment of your body, psyche, and spirit, as well as to those of your uborn. Healthy eating is just one aspect of the Leclaire Method.

GETTING THE RIGHT NUTRIENTS
FOR MOTHER AND UBORN

Once you become pregnant, your nutritional needs increase. It is advisable to take a prenatal vitamin with all requirements in one pill. This ensures that you will receive the nutrients necessary for yourself and for a healthy baby. The easiest way to prevent birth defects of the brain and spinal cord is to take a daily vitamin tablet of 400 micrograms of folic acid. Iron intake needs to be maintained at 15 milligrams daily. You can receive this from your food or in pill form as ferrous sulfate. You should discuss these needs with your certified nurse midwife or obstetrician.

I recommend that women begin taking prenatal vitamins three months prior to conception, if possible, and for three months to four years postpartum, until cessation of breastfeeding. You may think that your body gets to rest after the baby is born, but you will need additional nutrients as you breastfeed. You will also need more energy to respond to the needs of a growing child. Most babies need attention throughout the day and night, and you may be deprived of sleep. Vitamins will help your body rebuild during these crucial times.

FOOD FOR A HEALTHY PREGNANCY

Although vitamins are important, they will not take the place of a healthy variety of foods—especially fruits, vegetables, and whole grains. Choose foods that provide nutrients and that you enjoy eating. Cooked foods are often easier to digest during pregnancy; eliminate or avoid canned and processed foods. Along with being nourishing and comforting for you and your uborn, food should be delicious, and eating it should be a pleasant experience. Always eat in a serene environment. Even at breakfast, a candle on the table adds a nice touch. It helps to calm and center the nervous system. Your digestion works at its best when you do not have any distractions while eating. Don't read, watch television, or work on the computer. Good and pleasant conversation is okay, and if you are eating alone, you can use the time for a form of meditation by focusing on the color, flavors, texture, and comfort of your meal.

The development of your uborn and her physical and mental well-being depend on the quality of your food intake. Just as the school you send your child to is not half as important as the environment of your uterus, so the growth your child receives after birth is less significant than the formation and growth and development that take place in your uterus.

RECOMMENDED DIET

My experience with pregnant women and in health care over the past fifteen years has led me to recommend to pregnant women a diet that combines principles of macrobiotics and ayurvedic eating theories. The purpose of a macrobiotic diet is "to create balance within ourselves and with our environment by adjusting our daily food and activity to harmonize with changing circumstances," according to Michio Kushi and Aveline Kushi, the founders of macrobiotics.[1] *Ayurveda* means simply "the science of life." This is a science of health and preventive medicine that has been practiced in India for the past five thousand years and continues to be used today. Ayurvedic nutrition is based on each individual's body type and includes dairy products, vegetables, fruits, lentils, grains, animal foods, condiments, seeds, and oils. It avoids fried foods and very salty or very hot and spicy foods and does not include refined sugar.

I have observed that these nutritional programs have the best long-term effect for a healthy and satisfied mother and a healthy

---

1. Michio Kushi and Aveline Kushi, *Macrobiotic Pregnancy and Care of the Newborn* (Tokyo: Japan Publications, 1983), p.71.

baby. The choices I am suggesting are based on a diet designed for optimal health for the human body, the macrobiotic diet. You may wish to read some of the books listed in the Resources section of this book to learn more about nutrition and the health of your body and baby. The following suggestions will help you incorporate a few simple changes into your normal eating patterns that can increase your comfort during pregnancy and enhance the future health of your baby. Later in this chapter, you'll find basic nutritional plans for daily eating. Keep in mind that these are goals, and you should always make your goals easier to meet than not to meet. Small steps are all that are necessary, so be gentle with yourself as you make small changes.

Main dish: The main part of your pregnancy eating plan should consist of whole grains and cereal. About 60 percent of your diet during pregnancy should be made up of these. By cereal, I don't mean instant or canned cereal, but actual grains that you cook. Some examples of whole grains are brown rice, millet, oats, corn, rye, and buckwheat.

Beans: About 10 percent of your diet should be beans of some sort. I recommend adzuki beans, chickpeas (also called garbanzo beans), lentils, and mung beans for regular use; you should try to eat one of these types of beans at least once each day. Occasionally, or about three times a week, these beans can be eaten: black-eyed peas, soybeans, kidney beans, pinto beans (such as in refried beans), lima beans, navy beans, and whole or split peas. Fermented bean products such as tofu or tempeh may also be eaten occasionally, about twice a week.

Soups: Soups are a convenient and great-tasting way to combine the two important food categories of whole grains and beans. For a healthy instant soup, use refrigerated miso paste. Add hot water, wait a few minutes, and you have the perfect snack or meal. Soups are best seasoned with natural miso paste (don't use dried or powdered miso), which is made with fermented grains and soy. Miso is a popular soup base in Japanese cooking and can be found in most markets. Use miso paste as a soup base, with vegetables, beans, and grains to be included daily.

Vegetables: About 25 percent of your daily food should be vegetables. There are three main types of vegetables: root or stem vegetables (carrots, burdock, daikon radishes, dandelion roots, radishes, onions, rutabagas, turnips, parsnips, sweet potatoes); ground vegetables (cauliflower; acorn, butternut, and hubbard squash; pumpkin); and green and white leafy vegetables (broccoli, brussels sprouts, bok choy, green cabbage, carrot tops, Chinese cabbage, cilantro, collard greens, daikon greens, kale, mustard greens, parsley, chives, turnip greens, watercress, leeks). It is best to eat at least one vegetable from each of these groups daily.

Supplementary foods: These foods can contribute to your overall good health but should be eaten in moderation. If you add up the numbers, 95 percent of your diet should consist of whole grains, beans, and vegetables. That leaves only about 5 percent for other foods. You do need more protein when you are pregnant, so eat small amounts of these important protein foods each day:

- White meat fish, such as flounder, halibut, sole, carp, haddock, trout, and other white fish
- Seeds, such as sesame, sunflower, pumpkin, and squash seeds

For beverages, choose spring water, bancha-twig tea, roasted barley tea, or peppermint tea.

Condiments should be umeboshi plum (eaten two to three times a week), sesame salt, sea vegetable powder, brown rice vinegar, ginger, and kombu. Use sesame or olive oil for cooking or salad dressings.

For calcium, macrobiotics recommends eating sea vegetables daily, and they are especially good in soups. Japanese and other specialty sections of most markets now carry sea vegetables. They include kombu, wakame, nori, dulse, arame, hijiki, Irish moss, and agar agar.

Ayurvedic nutrition is based on the belief that individuals should consume food from each of six different taste categories every day. These categories are sweet, sour, salty, pungent, bitter, and astringent. During pregnancy, women should particularly savor the sweet, the sour, and the salty. *Sweet foods* include milk, butter, ghee, sweet fruits (such as raisins, dates, mangoes, pears, sweet pineapple, sweet berries, and sweet apples), sweet vegetables (such as sweet potatoes, carrots, cauliflower, and string beans), and most grains (such as rice, millet, whole-grain bread, and pasta). *Sour foods* include yogurt and ricotta or cottage cheese. *Salty foods* are anything containing salt. *Pungent foods* include mild spices, such as cinnamon, cardamom, fennel, or—in slight amounts—ginger. *Bitter foods* include spinach, green cabbage, kale, and chard. *Astringent foods* are beans, lentils, yellow split mung beans, and tofu. Ayurvedic nutritionists also highly recommend blanched almonds, which are particularly nourishing for the uborn. (Soak five almonds in water overnight and eat with breakfast.)

BALANCE IN EATING AND HEALTH

Be sure to eat a variety of foods. You may need more or different types of food—your fuel—depending on the amount of physical activity you do each day. Naturally you must adjust your foods within the framework of the macrobiotic diet to your climate and your workload.

As with all the recommendations and suggestions you will read in this book and elsewhere during your pregnancy, you must find a balance. If you are accustomed to eating a diet high in dairy and meat products, you might be dissatisfied if you change those habits overnight. Try using these macrobiotic guidelines a few days each week, even if you crave sweets or other foods. I think you'll find that you feel better and have more energy the more closely you follow this diet. But no one is perfect, and you'll have certain comfort foods that you don't want to give up. Balance these indulgences with healthier meals, and you'll still see the benefits of eating this way.

WORLD HEALTH ORGANIZATION RECOMMENDATIONS

Although I believe that the ayurvedic or macrobiotic diet offers the best approach to a lifetime of health for mother and child, keep in mind that opinions about what is best for mother and uborn vary. No one can change everything overnight. Your goal should be to establish healthy habits slowly and to incorporate as many of the foods as you can in your diet. If the macrobiotic or ayurvedic approach seems too extreme for you, try the following diet recommended for mothers-to-be by the World Health Organization (WHO), the global organization that monitors health. This diet includes the following daily (each serving is one-half cup):

- Three servings from the milk, yogurt, and cheese group
- Three to five servings from the vegetable group
- Two to three servings of meat, poultry, fish, dry beans, eggs, or nuts
- Two to four servings from the fruit group
- Six to eleven servings of bread, cereal, pasta, rice, or other grains

DAILY MENU IDEAS

To give you an idea of how these healthy eating guidelines might work in your daily life, I've put together the following menu suggestions. These suggestions are to coincide with the goals you'll be setting each week for your pregnancy. If you try some of these simple suggestions, you'll probably find it easier than you thought to eat healthy foods, and you'll find yourself enjoying them more than many of the foods you may be eating now.

Start by looking at your current diet. Suppose it is something like the following:

Mother's Basic Nonhealthy Diet

- *Breakfast:* coffee and a doughnut
- *Lunch:* hamburger, fries, and cola
- *Dinner:* pastrami on rye deli sandwich with pickle; cream soda

This diet may be at the extreme end of the spectrum, but it helps make the point. I know from my own life that the best way to adopt healthier habits is to do it gradually—one small change at a time—so adjust your diet with a few foods. Vowing to change your diet "tomorrow" rarely works. Choose a few healthy foods, in addition to whatever foods you are now eating, each day. Slowly you'll discover a vitality that will make you want to change to healthier eating. (The one change you *should* make right away, though, is to stop consuming caffeine and alcohol. These can harm your uborn.)

First Trimester

Add these foods, eating them before you eat the regular food you've been eating, such as the "junk" food listed in "Mother's Basic Nonhealthy Diet." Eat all those foods as you have been doing, deleting nothing except the coffee and cola. Perhaps choose a decaffeinated blend and a soda without caffeine and artificial sugar, the additives found in diet drinks.

- *Breakfast:* one cup cooked oatmeal (not instant)
- *Lunch:* one glass soymilk
- *Dinner:* one stalk broccoli, two carrots, collard greens

Second Trimester

Add these foods, eating them before you eat the regular food you've been eating, such as the "junk" food listed in "Mother's Basic Nonhealthy Diet." Eat all those foods as you have been doing, deleting nothing.

- *Breakfast:* one cup soymilk, one cup cooked oatmeal
- *Lunch:* one sweet potato and black bean burrito, kale
- *Dinner:* broccoli, asparagus, and grilled tofu or white fish

Third Trimester

Add these foods to what you are eating already during the third trimester. Keep in mind that the goal is to slowly change your habits to healthier ones.

- *Breakfast:* one cup oatmeal or other grain, one glass soymilk, two dates, one tablespoon sunflower seeds
- *Snack:* one-half cup cooked pears or applesauce
- *Lunch:* one piece grilled white fish, one-half cup cooked cauliflower, one-half cup cooked collard greens
- *Snack:* one cup miso soup
- *Dinner:* one-half cup broccoli, one-half cup cooked carrots, one cup mung bean and lentil dahl with basmati rice
- *Snack:* one cup boiled cow's milk (cooled to taste) with pinch of cardamom

The changes you're making are minimal. Just remember: Move toward a healthier diet every week and change something to a healthier food if you can.

FOOD PREFERENCES

By the third or fourth month of pregnancy, the uborn's heart is completely developed. Once the mother has two hearts, she may experience cravings. According to ayurvedic medicine, once the uborn's heart begins to beat, cravings should be satisfied. They are the cravings of the uborn, and there may be something in the desired food that helps to balance her constitution, which may be different from the constitution of the mother.

The Leclaire Method is about mindfulness and about paying attention to your own mind/body. Many women have found that if they simply pay more attention to how they feel after eating, they are drawn to eat healthy foods. For example, we've all experienced the high of a sugar rush on an empty stomach followed by the dip in energy in a short time, and possibly a headache accompanying this. Is this how you wish your baby to feel? Compare that to the way you feel after eating a balanced meal: a bowl of miso soup, steamed vegetables and rice, a bowl of fresh vegetable and tofu soup, or a steaming dish of red beans or lentils and rice. Think about the crispy apples in fall or delightful pears in winter. All of these foods can provide energy and nutrients, and you'll be happy you ate them later.

Listen to your own body. No one expects or wants you to give up all your favorite foods, even if they aren't good for you. But you'll feel better if most of your foods are from the lists suggested here.

THINGS TO AVOID

There are a few things mothers should avoid during pregnancy. It almost goes without saying that the mother should not have cigarettes, alcohol, caffeine, or other drugs (legal or illegal) during pregnancy. These can all be addictive to the child and may cause health problems at birth or after. (Because emotional drugs can harm a uborn as well, even violent television or movies should be avoided.)

Substance abuse during pregnancy puts both mother and uborn at risk. Such abuse puts babies at risk for low birth weight, congenital anomalies that can cause health problems throughout the child's life, mental retardation, neonatal abstinence syndrome (caused when the mother has been drinking alcohol and the baby is no longer receiving it because she has been born), attention deficit disorder, and prematurity anemia.

Other characteristics and complications of alcohol and drug use during pregnancy are too numerous to list here. In essence, the reproductive casualties for children prenatally exposed to drugs range from fetal death and spontaneous abortion to premature birth, intrauterine growth retardation, mental retardation, and learning problems.[2] (For help with substance abuse, call the Alcoholics Anonymous local listing in your telephone directory; the National Council on Alcoholism and Drug Dependence, 800-NCA-Call or 800-632-3255; or Narcotics Anonymous, 818-780-3951.)

Moving Through Pregnancy

Any health book you read will tell you that exercise must be part of any health program. Many women fear harming their uborns by exercise, but you can't stop moving altogether. Exercise increases circulation and keeps the metabolism functioning. Gentle movement done regularly is an essential part of your pregnancy health plan. Before you became pregnant, you may have exercised six times a week at the local gym, run every day, or done absolutely no physical exercise. As you go through pregnancy, you may need to adjust your exercise habits. Running doesn't work as your belly grows with the uborn, and doing no exercise should not be an option either. Instead you should find simple movements that help keep your muscles toned and your blood cells oxygenated. Exercising brings much-needed oxygen into your lungs, your blood, and your uborn. Gentle movements can also help your body use oxygen and food more efficiently.

---

2. J. Howard, "Developing Strategies for Educational Success." *School Safety* (Winter 1992).

Your blood volume increases significantly during pregnancy, and this can cause swelling of the veins. Daily exercise can help to prevent this swelling, and exercise also improves overall circulation. You should exercise at least twenty minutes daily to receive these benefits. Increasing your heart rate by walking briskly, swimming, or using a stationary horizontal bicycle (which is more comfortable for your back than a vertical bicycle) will improve your overall health and well-being. Outdoor exercise is the best because of the fresh air. Being outside provides oxygen, vitamin D from the sun, and other benefits of being in nature, such as the caress of a breeze or the scent of flowers. Yoga is another good exercise for pregnancy. It can help stabilize your mood, increase circulation, and prepare your body for labor. I usually suggest walking, yoga, or another nonimpact exercise for mothers-to-be.

Moving about through simple exercise will increase your energy during pregnancy (or at any time). Our bodies need movement and fresh oxygen to perform at their best. You may want to incorporate the following specific exercises into your health plan. They will help prepare certain muscles in your body for their role in childbirth. Combine them with a few simple stretches, and you will be training your body for one of its most important tasks: bringing a new life into the world.

EXERCISE: THE KEGEL MUSCLE

The Kegel muscle extends from the pubic bone to the tailbone, or coccyx. This muscle supports your uterus, vagina, rectum, and bladder. By strengthening this muscle, this exercise will help to ensure good bladder and bowel control.

Begin by stopping and starting the flow of your urine midstream while you are sitting on the toilet. After you are comfortable with this exercise, practice it when you are not urinating. Practice this contraction and relaxation at least ten times a day in sets of five.

EXERCISE: WIDENING THE BIRTH CANAL

These basic stretching exercises are good preparation for birth. Practice them daily to help widen your birthing passage. You may wish to expand the number of exercises you do. If so, consult one of the many good books and videos for yoga during pregnancy.

LYING LEG STRETCH: Rest on your back, with your legs straight out to your front. Make your legs as long as you can. Then, one leg at a time, bend at the knee and bring your leg up to your abdomen. Stretch the leg out straight again and bring the other leg up, with bent knee, to your abdomen. Straighten and stretch the leg. Then bring both legs, with knees bent, up to your abdomen, and then stretch and extend your legs again.

SITTING LEG STRETCH: Sit on the floor with your legs straight and wide apart. Sit with your lower back against a wall for support. Extend your legs in front of you, and again spread them as wide apart as you can. Close your eyes and send your exhalation out through your cervix and your vagina. Lean forward, touching the ground lightly with your hands and sending your exhalations down your spine and into the floor. Move back to sitting up and massage your thighs and knees gently.

KNEELING STRETCH: Kneel on a rug or mat, sitting back with your buttocks resting on your feet. Become aware of your breaths. Slowly move forward from your hips, keeping your spine straight. Place your palms on the floor, leaning forward. If you can do it comfortably, rest your elbows on the floor with your forearms and hands also resting on the floor. Gently lengthen your spine, and if you are comfortable doing it, move forward with your arms completely outstretched in front of you, resting with your forehead on the floor. Relax and breathe gently. Come up very slowly, supporting yourself as you did going down.

SQUATTING: Squatting daily for a minute or two is wonderful preparation for birthing. The only reasons not to do this are if you have hemorrhoids or painful varicose veins. If you don't know whether you should or should not squat, discuss it with your midwife, doctor, or other health care professional. *Caution:* If your uborn is in breech position, do not continue to practice squatting. Instead, practice the "all-fours position" (in position as if you were going to crawl), kneeling, with your chest resting on the floor or on your folded arms. These positions may help to turn a breech or posterior uborn.

OTHER STRETCHES FOR BIRTHING: Sitting on the toilet with a child's stool on either side, place your feet on the stools. This prepares your body for labor and is a comfortable position to use during labor. This exercise is particularly important during the last three weeks of your pregnancy. During the last three weeks, practice it two or three times each day for a minute at a time. The position encourages ease for you and enables the uborn to be in a good position for birth.

A Word of Caution

If you use a yoga book or video for pregnancy, do not try the inverted (upside down) positions. Some yoga teachers recommend these positions, but I do not. Dr. Vasant Lad, an ayurvedic physician experienced in working with pregnant women, also does not recommend inverted positions during pregnancy.

SEX AND THE EXPECTANT MOTHER

Many women feel that they may lose their husband if they don't satisfy his sexual desires and needs during pregnancy. Yoga and meditation for both mother and father are helpful for responding to sexual desires. These can help "color" desire, calming certain urges and allowing a calmness to permeate your time together so that your sexual desires together can become balanced.

The father should respect his partner and child and not seek other women to "satisfy" him during this time. Sometimes sexual relationships will be altered during pregnancy because of desires. Talk to your partner and be aware of your own needs and desires. The father can use extra energy to practice yoga or meditation or simply find ways to cuddle and support the mother. She in turn needs to trust her husband. Their current sexual needs should be discussed in a calm, loving manner. The father's job during pregnancy is to create happiness and joy.

Chapter Six

THE UMBILICAL CODE

A Feast for the Senses for Mother, Father, and Child

Until very recently, we assumed that the environment in the uterus was dark, warm, and silent, much like a cave in the deep bowels of Earth. The child in the womb was separate from the outside world, it was believed, and that world did not penetrate the protective surroundings of the amniotic sac and the mother's skin and tissue.

Recent studies have revealed that this assumption is wrong and that, in fact, the intrauterine world of the child is subject to changes caused by both the uborn's own growth and the actions in the world outside the mother's body.[1] Other research has shown that all human senses are actually working to some degree by the time the uborn is in the second trimester of development. Tests have shown that the uborn will respond to pressure, touch, heat, movement, sound, pain, and even certain types of taste.

---

1. For more information about the studies done and the evidence found, see Alessandra Piontelli, *From Fetus to Child* (London: Routledge, 1992), and Thomas Verny, *The Secret Life of the Unborn Child* (New York: Dell Publishing, 1981).

Your uborn's environment shifts with the stimuli—including sights, odors, sounds, tastes, and touch—that you experience during pregnancy. Uborns contribute to this environment themselves, shifting in the womb; "playing" with their fingers or bodies; and pushing with arms, legs, or head. The amniotic fluid changes during the course of pregnancy, too. Depending on your diet and the release of hormones in your body, the fluid's chemical makeup alters. During the last trimester, the uborn may swallow and excrete this fluid, again changing the composition of his environment.

Do perceptions experienced regularly during pregnancy, even before the brain develops, affect the cell development of the body, which in turn perhaps affects the structure of the emerging brain? These are important considerations when it comes to deciding how to care for yourself while you are creating a new life and a world for your baby.

So we can ask ourselves: How does the emotion of the mother communicate to the uborn, and how does it influence the development of the body/brain/mind and the adapting skills of the infant? How can and does the brain/mind of the uborn integrate the experience of the mother in a way that begins to shape a healthy, well-adapted, well-bonded infant?

NATURE VERSUS NURTURE

The correct environment is necessary to bring out the best and diminish the worst in the constitution and personality of a child's genetic makeup. The proper intrauterine environment and mother–father–child extrauterine interaction are necessary to enhance the best of a child's temperament and to contain the worst. A basic genetic makeup appears to be neither good nor bad; it just is. What is important is the effectiveness or ineffectiveness of the child's developmental environment in relation to her basic personality.

Even during pregnancy, be aware of the needs of not only you and your uborn, but also any other children you may have. Keep in mind that these needs change and that each child is different, even in the womb. What is good for one child may not be healthy for another. When you realize and implement this, it could create havoc in a household. One child might ask, for example, "Why do I have to go to bed earlier? I'm older," or "Why can't I run and jump for more than fifteen minutes? Why do you pay the babysitter to take Karen outside to encourage her to run and jump?"

As the socialist philosophy goes, "each according to his needs" or, in the vernacular, "different strokes for different folks." The question is knowing what is right for each mother–infant dyad and following through on the proper schedule, balanced diet, nursing style, and so on. All babies need structure and respect, but some need more structure; some need you to listen more.

All is potentiality: genes, metabolism, personality traits. It is the environment that creates the actualization and tho proper balance of infinite possibilities. As parents, we cannot relinquish responsibility to genetics. We must take charge and create the proper environmental influences.

But do we really need more responsibility and something else to feel guilty about? Just when we women are finally out there in the workforce, science is telling us how very, very important our role as mothers is. To prevent violence, we need to address it before its onset. The best money the government could spend to prevent future violence would be to create free prenatal development education centers and to pay mothers to breastfeed.

To gain some insight, we might look at the laboratory research, where psychobiologist Robert Cairns has given us vital information about aggressive behavior in mice. When a genetically aggressive mouse is being overreactive and edgy, Dr. Cairns reports, another mouse in contact with it can influence the aggressor so that it backs off rather than making an all-out attack. The second mouse, the nonaggressive mouse, accomplishes this change by freezing motion and not responding to the aggressor. Dr. Cairns states, "It's not a gene or a biochemical ... behaving but an integrated organism behaving within a real world."[2]

In other words, neither the genetic makeup nor the past history of the mouse is stopping its aggression. At least in part, its actions are determined by the response it has received. Dr. Cairns continues, "On the interim of the organism the success or failure of behavioral accommodation in reducing the threat and promoting well-being is recorded in the language of neurochemistry and hormones."

Breastfeeding is social interaction at a primal level. If our actions, like the mouse's, have a large behavioral component, you might say that breastfeeding is the mother's lab of gene/environmental interaction. The World Health Organization stresses, for example, that every child should be breastfed until six months of age, as part of the environment she is born into. Here you can observe daily your baby's interaction with mother and mother's interaction with baby. What do you need to be in balance? What does your infant need, and how can you both be in balance together? Where do you need to shift so he can shift comfortably? What escalates undesirable behavior, and what diminishes it? Just as with the mouse, the social behavior of your infant is in a perpetual state of development as it relates to you and your actions.

A FEAST FOR THE SENSES
OF MOTHER AND BABY

The structure of the brain is formed by interpersonal experience. As a product of the brain activity, the mind emerges. Of concern in this process is how the mother's experiences while pregnant

---

2. Debra Niehoff, Ph.D., *The Biology of Violence* (New York: The Free Press, 1999), 252.

and her perception of her past experiences affect the physical, emotional, and behavioral development of the uborn. Is there an umbilical code, an interpersonal relationship between the mother and her developing child that announces how a particular mind/ body interaction of the mother affects the specific areas of the brain/mind/body of the uborn and his subsequent interaction with the world?

Each of us is genetically programmed, but what is it that organizes that material in us individually? Various experiences and energy in the form of biochemical messages flow between mother and infant. How do these experiences and perceptions translate and perhaps transform the nervous system of the uborn? Perhaps each mother is not only growing a body/brain but also creating the mind of her uborn.

Let us look at a definition. *Merriam Webster's Collegiate Dictionary* defines *mind* as "1. recollection, memory; 2a. the element or complex of elements in an individual that feels, perceives, thinks, wills, and especially reasons; b. the conscious mental events and capabilities in an organism; c. the organized conscious and unconscious adaptive mental activity of an organism; 3. intention, desire; 4. the normal or healthy condition of the mental faculties; 5. opinion, view; 6. disposition, mood; 7a. a person or group embodying mental qualities; b. intellectual ability."

Although we don't know how, exactly, we do know that when the uborn's brain is developing, the mother participates in the activation of neurons, or electrical activity in the brain. The flow of energy in the mother's brain affects the flow of energy in her uborn's brain. In the fourth week of gestation, your uborn's cranial nerve motor neurons are forming. These control the muscles of the eye lens, throat, and tongue. Amazingly, this can occur even before a mother knows she is pregnant. The stem of the brain and your uborn's ears are simultaneously developing. At what crucial time in development are the mental processes of the uborn being established? We learn through our senses and perceive through our senses.

It is conceivable that each of the mother's sensory perceptions interacts with fetal development, but it is also conceivable that the interaction of the senses establishes a pattern of neural firing. Imagine, for example, that a mother is driving along in Malibu and passes the septic tanks there, with their intermittent bad odor. This smell could lead to a particular neural firing, if paired with a memory such as Frank McCourt describes in his book *Angela's Ashes* of growing up poor in Ireland near the public toilet. The smell could mean something different, however, depending on the mother's thoughts at the time. She might instead think, "Oh! I'm halfway home. Look at the waves; they're perfect. In twenty minutes I'll be in my wetsuit surfing. Isn't it funny how we all put up with the periodic stench of Malibu just to live here in such incredible beauty?"

As you can see, these are very different thought patterns, and very different neural firings could take place. How would each affect the neural firing of the mother and her uborn? Even before the brain develops, these perceptions, experienced regularly during pregnancy, may affect the cell development of the fetal body, which in turn perhaps affects the structure of the emerging brain.

Although these thoughts may seem quite theoretical to you, they are important for deciding how you are going to care for yourself while you are creating a new life and a new world. As explained in Chapter Two, you cannot control every thought you think during pregnancy, nor can you control many aspects of your environment—but you can control the way you *react* to thoughts and the environment. You can work to make the environment better for your uborn by controlling your reactions to the things you see, hear, smell, touch, and eat.

AVOIDING THE EMOTIONAL
ROLLER COASTER FOR YOUR UBORN

Perhaps we do not understand fully how the emotions of the mother communicate to the uborn, but we do know they communicate. These emotions, and especially the mother's response to them, influence the development of the body, the brain/mind, and the adapting skills of the infant. How does the brain/mind of the uborn learn to integrate the experience of the mother in a way that begins the shaping of a healthy, well-adjusted, well-bonded infant? We know that maternal deprivation after birth affects how the infant will deal with stress in the future. Is there a possibility that a mother not bonding with her developing uborn will have a similar effect? The latest studies on adoption tell us that if a mother bonds with her uborn in utero and subsequently puts her baby up for adoption, the baby is less stressed than if the mother does not bond. In other words, the baby needs bonding and needs to learn through the emotions of her mother, and this experience will help the baby even if the mother is not present with the baby after birth.

REMEMBERING AND CONNECTING
THROUGH STORIES

One way to come to grips with negative feelings and emotions and to avoid letting them control or destroy you is to integrate them through the use of story. I have used this method effectively with many mothers-to-be. The first step in the process is to view your past as a narrative and to tell that narrative the way it was, with all its hurts. It is then important to write it the way it was. You may not only write the story for yourself but also compose letters to parents or to others. In these letters, address your issues in a very real way. Do not send the letters; write them to address the issues in your own mind/body, not for confrontation. Next, it is important to rewrite the narrative with compassion and understanding of all of the players, including yourself. Forgiveness must be attained. Read that final narrative aloud to yourself three times and aloud to another person. Tape yourself as you read your story aloud so that you can replay it for yourself. Each of these steps is important and must be done. Retelling the story and examining it in this way will help you see that your perception of your story is more important than the actual content.

Using this method is especially critical if you had a troubled childhood or if you want to avoid repeating issues about your own parents and their treatment of you. Your perception of your past will affect your relationship with your own child. You can decide to be different from your own parents. You can decide to keep the good and delete the bad. Attachment studies show, however, that you will not be able to do this unless you change your brain patterns of remembering. Do the work. It's simple and effective. Our purpose is to find joy, to give joy, to share joy—not to wallow in our past lives of misunderstanding and pain.

We need to rework our pain into something constructive in order not to let the bad things that have happened to us take over our lives. Our feelings are a result of our thoughts; the meaning we attach to our thoughts gives rise to healthy or unhealthy feelings. Hurt and anger can be healthy or unhealthy depending on how these emotions affect our present interpersonal relationships. It is appropriate and healthy to be angry and hurt and to want to castrate your rapist and to want him prosecuted under the law. It is not healthy after three months of intensive healing work to give him power over your daily thoughts. As one woman said, "That man had power and control over one night of my life. I will never consciously let him have power and control over another moment." This narrative needs to be done in the same way that your childhood narrative was done in order to heal. It is important to use this scientific information we have learned about the brain to help us to heal and to help us to create healthy children and healthy families. Forgiving the rapist does not mean that you shouldn't want him to get life imprisonment. It just means that you need to try to understand that his past and his perception of his story made him the way he is. If he could have chosen differently, he would have. His behavior should receive the appropriate consequences, and your trauma needs to be addressed, redressed, and addressed and redressed and addressed and redressed, until you are complete and whole, happy and joyous again—even if for the first time in your life.

The way to integrate your internal and external worlds so that you can function as a happy and healthy compassionate human being is not through your emotions but through your perceptions of your experiences (which become your thinking) and your thought patterns (which result in responses that are your emotions).

When mother and father heal their past, they can create a new cognitive umbilical code that can establish an initial healthy formation of brain structure/functioning in their uborn. The baby can emerge as a healthy integration of the now cohesive past of the mother and father. Now the uborn becomes the embryonic reorganization of the mother's and father's past and his own present. This gives the baby a chance to emerge with a clean emotional and genetic slate.

The form and the material sent neuronatally need to be in harmony with the genetic intent of the uborn. How do we know what that is? Is the genetic code healthy in the first place? If so, how can the umbilical code enhance the genetic code, and how can it detract from it? Can the umbilical code alter the genetic code of subsequent generations? These questions are now arising based on the latest scientific knowledge. Our job is to do the best we can with the information we have at hand. By doing this, we can move in the direction of healing one step at a time. In the present, we must be gentle with ourselves and each other.

WORKING WITH YOUR SENSES

By following the methods outlined in the Leclaire Method, you will work with both your mind and your body to create the best environment for your baby. You will work with your mind through meditation and through the exercises described for changing your thoughts; you will work with your body through healthy eating and movement to provide the best for your uborn. At the same time, you should also nourish the senses of both yourself and your uborn. This is the fun part, the joy that comes from balance and harmony. By indulging in a few simple, sensual pleasures, you will be helping your uborn make the very most of both nature and nurture, and you will have a healthier, happier baby. The communications you share with your uborn begin now, and they include everything you see, touch, eat, hear, smell, and do during the months when your uborn shares your body. Use this time to indulge your own senses, learn ways to comfort yourself and your uborn, and discover ways to find joy in your surroundings each and every day. All of your senses need comfort and enjoyment during pregnancy and labor. For a detailed discussion of the sense of touch, see Chapter Eight, and for hearing, see Chapter Nine.

The Sense of Sight

During pregnancy, you should find as many ways as possible to look on beautiful sights. Watch happy movies; view art; gaze out your window at trees and flowers. Try to avoid sad news and sad movies. You want to deliver the best feelings and emotions possible to your uborn. Never watch television news, which seems to thrive on the most violent and horrific crimes and disasters. In addition, the news footage often shows more than we wish to see. This violence, and the fear and horror that come from watching others suffer, can cause a strong emotional response. Your response to the stress that you see on the news can cause an increase in adrenaline that in turn decreases the blood flow to the uterus and the placenta. You can, of course, stay informed by listening to radio stations that don't thrive on violence, traffic reports, and disasters. You can also read selective newspapers and magazines.

I once worked with a woman who was a uborn when her mother found out that her father had been killed by the Nazis. She was a delightful woman who channeled her chronic anxiety through her creativity. She felt as though she could never be completely at ease, however, even when she alone felt as though there was a storm brewing. She experienced a sense of impending doom and an underlying depression that she believed she "caught," like a systemic disease, from her mother. Her basic constitution was of high energy, and she had joie de vivre. Yet she believed that she needed an exorcism of sorts, that she was tainted in utero by her mother's severe shock and subsequent depression. This severe shock was not hers, yet somehow "it" resided in her cells. Her awareness of this helped her to live in conscious denial, and thus she could avoid letting it take her over.

No mother can be blamed for sights that she must confront during her pregnancy, and my coworker's mother should not be blamed for the sorrow and pain she felt. The story helps to illustrate why we must be as diligent as possible to view only those things that can uplift our spirits, however—especially during pregnancy.

The Sense of Taste

Since your uborn receives nourishment from you, everything you eat directly affects his health. (See Chapter Five.) Your food intake nourishes you, your uborn, and the development of your breast milk.

Ayurvedic medicine recommends balancing your body and acknowledging your cravings, especially during pregnancy, by satisfying your taste buds according to the six basic tastes: sweet, sour, salty, pungent, bitter, and astringent.

One should eat all of these tastes at each meal during pregnancy. Some healthy examples include:

Sweet: almonds, rice, milk, peppermint tea, honey, rice pudding, ghee, dates, raisins, barley, carrots, mullet, oats, melon, yellow squash

Sour: plain, unsweetened yogurt; cottage cheese; panir (Indian cheese)

Salty: sea salt, miso soup

Pungent: garlic, onion, celery seed (good for nausea), ginger, cumin, cinnamon, black pepper, anise seed

Bitter: rhubarb, turmeric, cumin, cinnamon, sesame seed, sesame oil, pumpkin

Astringent: green leafy vegetables, broccoli, cauliflower, cabbage, celery, lentils, mung beans, soybeans

The Sense of Smell

Gentle Fragrances, Soothing Scents

Aromas, like other sensory input, can be therapeutic to your well-being. It is the sense of smell that most often triggers a remembrance of things past, as French novelist Marcel Proust so aptly demonstrates in his amazing novel of the same name. Aroma is used intentionally during pregnancy and labor to relieve stress and to relax the mother. In addition, aroma can be used during labor to alter the perception of contractions. The use of scent can be a sort of conditioning. When we inhale the molecules of odor, they trigger the olfactory nerve, which can bring about physiological and emotional change. The change we are looking for is a deepening of the relaxation response, a relaxation of the breath, and a feeling of well-being.

Many scents are comforting, but one of the simplest to purchase or make is rosewater. (To make this scent, simply soak rose petals in water overnight.) The scent of rose encourages calm breathing, uplifts the spirit, and releases anxiety. Begin to use this scent in early pregnancy. Use it after you have practiced your hypnosis tapes or after meditating. The scent itself is relaxing, and when you pair it with an already relaxed state, it can double your relaxation. You can put a few drops of the rosewater scent on a cotton ball and hold it in front of your nose in your cupped hands. You can also put a few drops in a diffuser or in a bowl of hot water. This method can easily be used to scent the labor room to wonderful effect. You will find the use of rosewater scent especially effective during transition.

Lavender and jasmine are also good scents to use during labor. Try the different aromas a few weeks before labor to decide which one you like and for what reason.

Scents Postpartum

For postpartum fatigue, rosewater, rose oil, orange oil, and lemon oil have helped many women. Put a few drops on a cotton ball and keep it nearby to elevate your mood. To make orange or lemon zest, finely grate the skin of the fruit into a saucer. Keep the saucer nearby and periodically enjoy the wonderfully clean and uplifting fragrance.

PLAYING FOR YOUR HEALTH
(AND FOR YOUR BABY'S HEALTH)

Play is important for your mental, physical, and spiritual health. Play helps you bond better with your baby. Best of all, play is any activity that is fun and not goal oriented and that enables you to be present in the now, in the moment. Play can be with another person—adult or child—but don't wait for someone else to "play" with; it is important to schedule play into your life on a daily basis. Don't make playing contingent on anyone else.

Discover ways to play each and every day. Here are a few examples of what "play" could be:

- Watching the clouds
- Watching birds
- Reading a book
- Playing a musical instrument
- Gardening
- Watching an entertaining film
- Playing with your uborn
- Blowing bubbles
- Reading to your uborn
- Building a sand castle
- Arranging flowers
- Watching patterns of light
- Singing
- Dancing to your favorite music

Chapter Seven

STARDUST MEMORIES

Dreaming Your Way Through Pregnancy

It is night; my mind sighs.
Exhaling into the night's chasm.
Dreams of a wild mustang.
I awaken briefly, you are next to me.
Another you, perhaps, growing inside me.
Or is it I that is being born again?
Dream me a Dream of ancient Dreamers.
Send me oysters and owls and olive branches.
Send me a baby bathed in sapphire and shells.

I wrote this poem about one of my own dreams. It illustrates what I believe about dreams: that they connect us both to our own beings and to the larger world. They connect us to our collective past and to our collective future. They are one way in which we all seem to communicate with the infinite.

Are the visions that occur to us when we sleep voluntary or involuntary? Are our dreams the products of our sleeping mind/body, as our urine is the product of our kidneys? We don't know the answers to these questions, but we do know that dreams can and do have a powerful effect on our minds and emotions. We also know that pregnancy can be a time of condensation of thoughts, ideas, and feelings, and these are often distilled into a series of dreams.

It would seem strange that our dreams are products of undirected chance. Since we have dreams, we can assume that they are present so that they can be of use to us. Dreams appear to be indicators of bodily and life states. They seem to indicate that something is wrong and needs to be improved or that something is right and needs to be maintained.

Each dream has its individual qualities of clarity, noise level, anxiety level, texture, depth, expectancy, temperament, place, climate, tense (present, past, or future), surroundings, and formations. Each dream is a vehicle used by the mind to maintain a homeostasis of body and equilibrium in the world. Many psychologists believe that dreams offer opportunities to solve problems so that we can flourish in our environment. They give us a new chance for transformation.

CONNECTING TO A LARGER WORLD

For many years, theorists and researchers have studied dreams and their meanings, both to individuals and to cultures. Each of us has dreams, perhaps independently of each other and for different reasons. Carl Jung, a Swiss analyst of the early 1900s, wrote of the collective unconscious, humankind's experiences that we continually replicate and that unconsciously predispose the shape of our dreams. He believed that thought patterns and symbols were universally present in all dreamers but that prototypes differ across cultures.

Are the animals in your dreams related to similar animals in the dreams of a Native Indian? Perhaps the origins of animal symbols in dreams sprang from a specific purpose or need. An original meaning, however, may have shifted to fit our present-day purpose. In practice, it doesn't seem to really matter what we think about the origin of symbols in the dream. What matters is that the symbols we choose are useful for the normal growth and development of the mother and her uborn. Are the symbols in dreams context dependent—or is a dog always a symbol of loyalty? The appropriate meaning finds its indicator in the climate of the dream and in the gradual balancing of the dreamer. Sometimes a dream doesn't even need to be understood if it establishes equilibrium in the dreamer without the dreamer's conscious participation. The unconscious strives for balance, just as the body is always balancing itself, toward a state of harmony.

Some mothers have come in after I haven't seen them for a few weeks and told me about a series of dreams, one linking directly to the next, and then a dream that seems to be greatly divided from the others. A great chasm abounds between three in the series and the fourth, for example. Through the mother's free association and the joint analysis of the dream, we build a ramp between mother and uborn, between mother and motherhood, between mother and her ability to enter a more complete state of well-being.

DREAMS IN YOUR WIDE-AWAKE LIFE

Native Indians believe that dreams are of great significance and that sometimes they are more significant than waking life. Some of the most important revelations for an individual can occur in her dreams. Plato believed that the art of dreaming means that the dreamer is present in the experience, not as a copy of the experience but as reality itself.

It is very appropriate to ask yourself to dream a dream that will answer a question you have been pondering. Dream incubation, which is asking your unconscious for a specific dream for guidance, for healing, or to answer questions relevant to the dreamer, is an efficient way of solving problems. This dream practice was used in ancient Egypt, Rome, and Greece. It is an effective way of penetrating your emotions to arrive at a somewhat disguised meaning and need. Perhaps this communication from the unconscious is less than clear in order to give us fallible humans a chance to live in denial a bit longer if we choose. It takes willingness and a bit of interpretation to arrive at the true meaning of the dream. It is my experience, however, that dream work is one of the best and most exciting and safe ways of dealing with conflicts. If we don't eventually pay attention to the message of the dream, I have observed, we will be overwhelmed in some way in our bodies and our lives.

One mother in her seventh month, for example, dreamed of a large needle with thread in a man's hand. She hadn't consciously asked for this dream, but she was feeling uncomfortable at the time about her obstetrician's dismissing her birth plan as a wish list that probably wouldn't be fulfilled. Her main desire was not to have an episiotomy. Instead of respecting her desire, her obstetrician kept telling her about the benefits of an episiotomy. This exchange was beginning to ruin her expectancy of a wonderful birth. After discussing the dream with me at length for two sessions, she finally decided to change doctors and to hire a certified nurse midwife (CNM). She succeeded in having the comfortable, easy birth that she desired, without an episiotomy.

BEING ATTENTIVE TO YOUR DREAMS WITHOUT JUDGING

The best way to deal with dreams is to maintain a compassionate point of view. Accept your dreams as an attempt to nourish you. Bring to your dream interpretation only observation; avoid all judgment. Judgment is pointless. Dreaming is just another state of consciousness. There is nothing to attack, only a need for defenseless understanding. In the center of the dream state is you, the witness, the gentle observer, the nourishing interpreter.

During pregnancy, be careful to prepare for restful sleep and lucid dreaming. Throughout the day, avoid tea, coffee, alcohol, and tranquilizers. Eat foods that are soothing to your body type and nourish your senses in a way that is comforting rather than stimulating to you and your baby.

Refrain from eating heavy meals, especially for three hours prior to sleep. Just before you go to bed, drink a cup of boiled milk (cooled to a comfortable drinking temperature) with nutmeg and cardamom. Then go to bed no later than 10 P.M.

THE PATH TO UNIVERSAL TRUTH

Through your dreams, you can connect your instinct with your life's plan. In dreams, you are free to roam outside the parameters set for you by parents, culture, or society. Perhaps you can roam even beyond the boundaries that you set for yourself in your waking life. In order to be fulfilled, we need to know what our nature is, to reconnect to that nature, and finally to strive toward achieving the full potential of our self. Often a conflict arises between what our true nature is and what has been imposed upon us. In dreams, you can become integrated; you can supply your own ideals and goals to the birthing process as well as to other areas of your life.

Your emotional association to your dream content can help you uncover the message of your dream. This is why it is some-times helpful to seek a professional analyst to help you interpret your dreams. The analyst can help you sort through the content to the emotion behind the content and your reaction to the dream. To better understand this, think of filmmaking: The dreamer is the writer; the instinct does the directing; the soul does the lighting and the photography; and the dream analyst or therapist joins the dreamer as coproducer, taking all the raw material, putting it together, and making from it a cohesive whole. We can even program ourselves to dream.

Much of our consciousness is at the raw, instinctive level. Along comes the world of time, minutes, days, each a new experience, maybe some very similar to the ones before. Through these experiences, an ever-changing state of being is imposed upon us, and sometimes our true consciousness is repressed. We begin to act as if we and the world's perception of us are one and the same. Our emotions, what we sometimes call our "gut reactions," still express our true consciousness. Through our dreams, we can come into contact with those emotions in a "safe" way. By being attentive to our dreams, we can integrate these true parts of ourselves into our waking life.

Case Study: Julie

Julie, a young woman who had breast cancer and whom I met while working at a weeklong cancer retreat, was able to program herself to dream and to find out what would make her happy. Julie had been successful in her own business and prominent in her community, and these things had fulfilled her need for autonomy and creativity. She had given this business up totally when she became a mother, however. She enjoyed her children and had a very good relationship with her husband, James.

Julie decided that she wanted to live, that she would do all in her power to participate with her life force. To do so, though, she knew that she would have to reconnect to her creativity, which she had not paid attention to since beginning her family. This thought tormented her, because she had no idea what she wanted to do. Her husband had just opened a paint supply store for Julie so she could get out of the house. Julie said it did fill her time, but she didn't know if it was what she really wanted to do.

I told her that an easy way to find out what she really wanted was to tell herself that she would like to receive an answer in a dream. During the retreat, we had three-hour lunch breaks so that patients and staff could rest, meditate, exercise, and/or do their assignments for the afternoon session. After one of these breaks, Julie had a big smile on her face, and her whole being seemed happy.

"I took a nap," she said, "and I had the dream. I know exactly what I want to do. I don't want any part of the store. I talked with James, and he agreed that we would close it ASAP. I used to paint, and I am going to set aside time each week to do that. Believe it or not, I am going to take ballet lessons. It's something I always thought about, but was afraid of."

Julie seemed to have a new freedom about her as we interacted during the remainder of the week. She had allowed her life force to take over, and it showed.

EGO, INSTINCT, SELF, AND THE DREAM

Through the process of acknowledging your emotions and their importance, and through associating them with dream fragments, you can begin to interpret your dreams. Through the interpretation of dreams, especially those in the last trimester, you are freed to give yourself full permission to birth your baby in a conscious, joyous manner. It has become apparent to me that a most significant dream usually emerges during the third trimester of pregnancy. This dream is inevitably the one that holds the core of the remaining fears and ambivalence of the mother.

A secure environment has already been prepared through dealing with the myths, drawing the pictures, and discussing your ambivalence. Now you are safely able to attend to your remaining psychological preparation for an easy birthing. In the Leclaire Method, a special session is scheduled whenever the mother chooses, usually during the last trimester, and the mother and therapist go extensively through all the mother's associations to each word, name, phrase, color—each nuance in the dream. An interpretation of the dream is then made and discussed. This takes approximately three to six hours and may be done in three two-hour sessions.

The mother usually feels relieved, excited, and free. Any depression that might be creeping up on her is usually worked through at this time. It has been my observation that the woman then has an entirely different pattern of dreaming; that is, her dreams become exciting and anticipatory in preparation for the coming event. Sometimes this third trimester dream is truly just the tip of the iceberg, however, and other problems and fears present themselves. The mother is usually eager and willing to work these through and looks forward to her dream work sessions. It seems as though the mind, body, and spirit are all striving for prebirthing alignment.

Just as the imminent birth of your baby affords you new hope and a reconnection to the life force, so the dream process reconnects you to your own inner life force. Working with the dream process during pregnancy becomes an exciting task. Every fiber of your being desires to be conscious for the birthing.

The awakening of the unconscious that invariably occurs in the third trimester of pregnancy calls forth a primitive defense reaction. Unless this defense system is addressed, aided, and assisted through an analysis of the dream material, the laboring woman records it as anxiety, fear, and pain. In consideration of this, prevention is essential. Christina's dream work illustrates this well.

Case Study: Christina

One mother, Christina, was attending birth classes with her husband, Thomas. They were both enjoying the classes and felt excited about having their second child using hypnosis.

During Christina's twenty-fifth week, however, her father was hospitalized for cancer, and her mother began to spend every waking minute at his side. Christina had many feelings about this, but she was not articulating them at that time.

At twenty-six weeks, Christina visited her obstetrician, who noticed an outbreak of herpes. It was Christina's first flareup in ten years. At twenty-seven weeks, her uborn had turned to a podalic (feet-first) position. If the uborn did not turn on her own, she would need assistance. If the herpes flared up and did not disappear, a cesarean section would be necessary.

Aware of the connection between mind and body, Christina came privately to discuss her feelings about her mother's being unavailable for her. She told me of her first birth, which her mother and father, her husband, and her sisters had all attended. She was worried that her father might not be well enough to attend this birth, and if he were not, her mother probably would not leave his side for long. Her four-year-old was going to be at the birth, and Christina's mom had previously agreed to be the support person to her granddaughter. This, too, would have to change.

After Christina talked about her feelings and drew a picture of herself and her herpes, we made a hypnotherapy and healing tape. After much discussion, we decided that the best way to get to the bottom of this was for Christina to record her dreams and listen to her tape daily. During that week, Christina had a dream, which she described thus:

"I was in a movie set on a patio area. Phil Donahue and Marlo Thomas were sitting on a bench beside a low white brick wall. There were small plants in large planters in a room. The set wasn't getting built, and the movie wasn't being made fast enough. All of a sudden, young (in their early twenties) men and woman came out dressed in military uniforms, but they weren't Nazis. They were taking people away. I had to do something. I realized I had no place to hide. Marlo and Phil were separated by a partition, and only their feet could be seen.

"A young man started to take me. I went over to a young woman, who started to frisk me, but didn't finish. I took her arm and told her, 'I want to go with my husband, Thomas.' Thomas then suddenly appeared. They were going to take him away. I took the woman's arm and went over to Thomas. I was really upset. I had to go with my husband. We went into a dark room like a theater. There was a man in his fifties or sixties, crying, and a woman sitting in the shadows. Something bad was going on in the room."

Together, we discussed Christina's associations and the analysis of the dream over a few sessions. Here is the "essence of the dream," as later written by Christina:

"Marlo Thomas and Phil Donahue represented people worthy of making a contribution. Marlo specifically represents someone who does what she wants to do and feels good about her contribution to the world. I have respect for Phil. He also does what he wants and has integrity, and they both represent financial security and success. I could see their feet under the partition. She wore heels and a skirt, and he had brand-new shoes and slacks. Their feet were on the ground, the way I want to feel and be. My father seemed to be the man weeping in the theater, and my mother was sitting in the shadow. I was relating to making some of the same mistakes that my father had made. One of the problems was having to be 'ill' as he had been.

"I realized that I do not want to manifest these problems of 'unworthiness.' I don't want to blindly follow my husband, as my mother did my father. I could break this pattern by staying conscious instead of walking into the darkness (unconsciousness). I am not my father. I am not my mother.

"Through my dream, I discovered why I was creating being ill during my pregnancy. Hypnosis and the dream work helped me to control my illness, so I did not have to have a cesarean section."

Within one week after the dream analysis, Christina's herpes had disappeared, and her uborn had turned around. Now the uborn was in the proper position for birth, and the mother felt ready to give birth. Two days after Christina's due date, I received a phone call from her. She was in the birthing room, and all was going well. We spoke briefly, interrupted by two contractions.

Christina's husband, her four-year-old, and her sister attended the birth. Her mother stopped by for a visit, as her father was now home and doing well. At one point during transition, Christina looked at the crowd and, seeing her family's mounting tension, half in jest and half creating the right environment, the right "self" for herself, she instructed, "Now, one-two-three, everyone take a deep breath and let it go. Relax."

Everyone laughed, and the tension subsided. Unmedicated and delighted, she birthed a healthy baby girl.

REMEMBERING AND TELLING YOUR DREAMS

Many women tell me that they can't remember their dreams. The first step toward remembering is desire. Ask yourself if you really want to remember your dreams and why. If you decide that you would like to remember them, get yourself into a hypnotic or relaxed state and begin to imagine an inner guide. The guide can take any form. There is no right or wrong image or sensation. Speak to yourself or to your guide and say that you want to remember your dreams.

When you awake in the morning, before you open your eyes or move about, ask yourself: "What did I dream?" Stay in the awakening position as you remember your dream. If you can't remember, focus your attention on the area between your eyebrows, often called the third eye, and relax into it. This can stimulate the fragments of your dream to the surface of your consciousness.

With your eyes barely open, reach for a pen and pad of paper and write the dream, even if all you have are fragments. Often, as you tell aloud or write the dream, more details come to mind. Do not judge your dream; simply record it.

INTERPRETING YOUR DREAMS

You may wish to consult with a dream analyst or some other person trained in understanding dreams. You can learn to interpret your own dreams, too, however, by paying attention to them. Begin by retelling the dream, and then choose the most confusing aspect of the dream. Write down anything that comes to mind when you think about the confusing part. Rapidly write the first thing that comes to mind. Approach every dream with childlike curiosity. (Some people find that talking with others about the dream works better.)

I have found that the starting point of dream interpretation is the actual telling of the dream. A second telling of the dream puts the dreamer into closer contact with the dream state. As the dreamer describes the content, the analyst visualizes all the images, thus becoming more in touch with the diaphanous fabric of the dream state. Once both dreamer and analyst are focused, the atmosphere is prepared, and the dreamer can begin active association. It helps to speak of the characters and the sets in the dream as though they were happening now. The analyst listens, never interrupting the flow, questioning only to uncover more material, talking only to further open the imagination and association.

Case Study: Dawn

Dawn (thirty-seven weeks pregnant) received great benefit from her dreams only after we worked together in a group atmosphere. A sculptor, Dawn had great difficulty expressing herself through two-dimensional media such as painting, drawing, or writing. She was having trouble associating to her dream content, so she wrote it down just after awaking, and then each person in the group read her dream aloud to her. With each reading of the dream, Dawn opened up a bit more. Here are the dream and some of Dawn's feelings about it. (Dawn knew that she was having a boy.)

"Last night I dreamt about holding our baby in my arms. She cuddled up to me for a while until she opened her eyes. They were the most beautiful gray eyes. We looked into each other's eyes with moments of ecstasy and love; then her beautiful eyes grew larger and opened wider, and she arched her back, trying to get away from me. Suddenly, she was about two and a half to three years old and wanted to be fed a bottle by her father. I felt so rejected by her hatred for me, which seemed to come out often. I chased her around the room, closing doors. She crawled under the chair, shrieking when I grabbed her legs."

After much work on the dream, both privately and in a group, Dawn made these comments:

"It was like looking into my own eyes as an infant and being both the mother and the infant at the same time. Emotionally, I was feeling both the mother's feelings and the infant's feelings simultaneously. I am not close to my own mother, nor to my sister now. I would like to heal our family and be closer to my mother.

"The furniture in the room, specifically my paternal grandmother's chair, holds a memory of a day when my dad was very sick, and he sat in the chair all night. When I was little, between ages four and eight, I was afraid that monsters were trying to pull me under my bed. I had a secret ritual that made me safe. I would put my legs out of bed, touch the chair and then touch my dad, and I would feel safe. When the mother in the dreams kept closing doors, it reminded me of a room I had as an adolescent; in that house, I had my own private exit. I felt comfortable in that room. I have a hard time being in a room if the doors and windows are shut.

"Then I began to feel sad and deprived of a nurturer, and I remembered Rose, a woman employed by my parents for housekeeping and to care for me. Rose worked hard all day, and then at night she would visit the sick in the hospital. She was involved in her church and was very religious."

As Dawn told this, she was wearing a wonderful, frilly dress covered in roses. When she first spoke of Rose, she began to cry. She realized her love for this woman and how much she missed her. "I had forgotten her," she said, weeping. Later, she said, "I feel I have been given a gift. The feelings of the rejection of the mother didn't feel so scary. I didn't feel so guilty. The other women shared their feelings about their mothers. They could all understand that the baby was afraid that her mother couldn't nourish her. I realized that it wasn't such a horrible reaction. It was understandable. I had been feeling guilty that I had been rejecting my mother and that I caused her pain. The other women [in the group] being so accepting made me feel less guilty. I feel more whole now. Yes, I was nurtured by Rose and my father and my mother, and now I feel confident that I can break that pattern of several generations of women in our family not being nurtured."

Case Study: Melissa

Another mother reported the following to me. She was pregnant for the second time and had had an abortion to terminate the first pregnancy. "In the dream, my pants filled up with thick blood, and I thought there was a small fetus in there. But it wasn't curled like pictures I'd seen of fetuses. It was straight and had arms and legs. I felt it represented my aborted baby. I call her Elizabeth.

"In the dream, I was trying to make it into the bathroom to the toilet. It was the automatic thing to do with such a mess. I woke up before I actually made it there, or maybe just as I made it to the toilet.

"I suppose I was going to get rid of all this stuff. I didn't know what else to do with it. I suppose I was going to flush it, but I woke up before that happened. Anyway, it was an awful lot of this congealed blood. The baby was small in size compared to all the blood that was there, and the blood was an odd texture, more like gelatin.

"Then, days later, while I was contemplating the dream, I saw and felt that the blob of blood was the sacred heart. The color and shape reminded me of that. Where can I go with that image? What should I know about the Sacred Heart in my life?"

My response to Melissa was this: "In your dream, you were giving birth to the child that you so much did not want to give birth to before. She had to come out so that you could confront the choice you made. To look at it squarely. There's less space in you now for things to hide. Your dream indicates that we can hide nothing from the Sacred Heart. He knows all there is to know about you, so there is no use in hiding things from yourself, no use in burying them. Just let out whatever needs to come out. It will lighten your load."

We worked together on this dream for many weeks. It illustrates something that comes up often for mothers. Even when a woman is certain she needs an abortion at some point in her life, it may later come to mind again. It frequently surfaces during a pregnancy that is wanted. It reemerges as a fear that she could be punished for having had the abortion by having a miscarriage this time.

Women need a lot of support and understanding around dreams such as this one. Sometimes we even do a ceremony for the aborted baby. First, the mother writes a letter to him, saying whatever needs to be said. Then we do a ritual together, or the mother goes off in nature and does the ritual alone or with her support person. This clears the path for the next baby and pregnancy. This also helps the passage of the next baby to be calm and easy and can prevent a prolonged labor.

EXERCISE: USING YOUR DREAMS

Bringing your feelings and your attitudes into conscious awareness cannot hurt you, but remaining in denial and fear can. Gently pat yourself on your back for being willing to take the risk of looking at your dreams. Good luck!

1. Decide to remain open and curious to your dreams.

2. Buy a special notebook for recording your dreams.

3. Decide when you would like to begin to remember your dreams.

4. On the date you have decided, have your notebook and pen or pencil next to your bed.

5. Follow the suggestions in this chapter for remembering and telling your dreams.

Chapter Eight

MAGIC FINGERS

THE HEALING POWER OF HYPNOTOUCH

Women's bodies are as beautiful and varied as the bodies of new babies, and women's bodies have something else in common with those tiny newborns: They are natural and have natural instincts for touching and moving that can heal and help them thrive. You'll want to explore the changes in your body that occur naturally with pregnancy. You'll want to share the movements of the uborn with your partner and perhaps with others, letting them place their hands on your skin, feeling the pressure of a baby foot or hand. You'll also want to be held and soothed by your partner. You'll want to move into different positions for sleeping or hugging, and you'll want to experiment with how it feels to be in different positions for labor. Pregnancy can teach you a great respect for your body and all the miraculous ways it creates life. Relish this time as a time to observe and become more attuned to how your body functions.

The power of touch can be used to ease your own body and connect with your uborn. Hypnotouch helps you to access states of consciousness that are helpful for morning sickness, hyperemesisgravidarum (uncontrollable nausea and vomiting), prenatal anxiety, hypertension, breech presentation, preterm labor, discomfort and painful contractions, and postpartum depression. It is important to note that the purpose of this book is not to help to heal these conditions but to prevent them in the first place.

Hypnotouch is both mindful and effortless. It requires desire on the part of the healer, inner stillness, a complete willingness to be present in the moment, an openness to your own sensitivity and intuition, and an openness to consciously using your mind and the healing energy of your body to balance disorders and discomforts in the mother. All the mother needs to do is be a willing participant. She needs to be willing to be healed, to be touched, skin to skin or skin to clothing, or without touching but just with healing and soothing or fluffing of the energy field around her body.

TRADITIONAL POSITIONS FOR EASIER BIRTHS

Our society is different from traditional societies when it comes to our attitudes and approach to pregnancy, birthing, and touch for mothers and their babies. Traditionally, women have lived in the framework of extended families and communities, where all supported each other and were interdependent. In these societies, the village truly helped to prepare the pregnant mother and then helped to raise her child. *In most societies throughout the world, before industrialization,* women depended on each other and on their own instincts for information about childbirth. In these societies, and among many women still living in these more traditional cultures, women birth in a squatting position and acknowledge the human tendency of touch as a basic human need.[1]

---

1. For more information about traditional birth practices in various cultures, please read *History of Childbirth* by Jacques Gelis and Rosemary Morris, translator (Boston: Northeastern University Press, 1991).

Squatting position: Squatting or crouching appears to be the most instinctive position for birth. This is the position used for defecation, which may perhaps be one reason it seems natural. It is often the urge a woman feels when she is about to give birth. These instincts should be adhered to, because squatting is the safest position for a woman giving birth alone; the uborn does not have far to fall if she appears suddenly. It is also a position in which the mother can most easily reach her perineum and disengage her baby's head, if necessary, and even catch her baby as she emerges from the birth canal.

Kneeling position: Kneeling is also an instinctive position and was frequently used until the end of the nineteenth century. A woman would often kneel between two chairs, supporting herself with one arm over each chair, or she could use two stools and have an arm over each stool. Her knees would be on the ground. A basket lined with straw was placed between the woman's widely spread legs to catch the baby.

All-fours position: Being on all fours, meaning on your knees and hands, like a four-legged animal, is a position still encouraged by midwives. You position yourself on your knees and then use your hands for additional support. Midwives have found this an effective position for mothers to use if the baby is not in the normal presentation position.

You should experiment with each of these positions and find which feels most natural to you before you enter labor. During labor, you should again move around and test the comfort of each of these traditional positions. You may feel that one position is better at one stage of labor and another at the next stage. The important thing is to know that your body may be the best "expert" about the optimum position for you and your baby. Just as your body knows how to "grow" a baby, it will help you find the right and comfortable position to bring the baby out into the world.

BODIES BUILT FOR BABIES

Another area in which we should observe more traditional societies and learn from their attitudes is that of touching our babies
and each other. In the early part of the twentieth century,
Western medical science began instructing women on the care of
their newborns, and much of this advice went against what had
often been common practice in families. In the 1920s, two books
were published that profoundly influenced new mothers and
their approach to their babies. These two books, *The Care and
Feeding of Children,* by Cannett Holt (New York: Health Services,
1924), and *Psychological Care of Infant and Child,* by John G.
Watson (New York: W. W. Norton, 1928), suggested that mothers
should touch their children less and give them less attention.
These books created a trend in American society that discouraged touching. Dr. Holt advised against picking up a baby and
holding him, saying that such care would spoil babies. Dr.
Watson built on this advice to suggest that mothers never hug or
kiss their babies. He instructed mothers not to let their babies sit
on their laps, not to pick up babies, and not to rock them. This
really was the advice given by the psychological childcare
experts of the day, even though it sounds ridiculous now. This
trend created fear and discomfort among mothers who were
inclined to heed their natural desire for physical contact with
their children.

It is a natural desire for a mother to keep her baby close to
her, to straddle her baby on the natural curve of her hips. Many
people believe that the curve of a woman's hip evolved so that
she could comfortably carry her baby on her hip as she went
about activities in her daily life. In preindustrial societies,
women held their babies as they worked, in most instances
planting or tending fields, cooking food, or gathering wood and
food for their families. The baby was comfortable with these
movements, in part because they were the same movements she

had experienced in the uterus. In those societies, women did not drastically curtail their activities or change their lifestyles during pregnancy.

Today, however, women try to make their hips as straight and as bony as possible—not a very comfortable place for a baby to be. Women of today with a desire for straight hips show how bodily desire can perhaps manifest an unconscious desire not to care for or carry a baby. Is it because we all grew up thinking that too much attention was bad for a baby because that is what the experts told us?

In fact, one of the best things we can do for our babies is to keep them near us during our activities and to let our bodies stay in close contact with their bodies. This eases a baby's transition from being part of his mother's body to becoming an individual, separate child. A baby who goes directly from the warm, protected environment of a womb to the cold, clinical "crib," no matter how much we've paid for the designer sheets, will not thrive.

HUMAN WARMTH
VERSUS MACHINE WARMTH

Although these childhood experts discouraged mothers from touching or pampering their newborns, another medical professional eventually reintroduced the power of touch to mothers. In 1938, loving touch "mothering" was introduced to American hospitals and institutions after an American physician visited a clinic in Germany. There, in one of the hospitals he visited, he observed an old woman carrying around a sick baby. The staff told him that they gave all their treatment "failures" to this old woman, Anna, and that she was always successful in helping them heal. The babies under Anna's care suffered what medical practitioners call *failure to thrive syndrome*. Babies with this condition are often seemingly healthy but just do not grow or absorb nutrients as expected. Although doctors can find no cause, these babies simply fail to thrive. In this German hospital, the attentions of Anna—mostly holding and carrying the babies as many hours a day as possible—seemed to overcome the failure to thrive syndrome. These babies eventually went home healthy.

After Anna's mothering touch was introduced and became common practice in America, the infant mortality rate in one hospital in New York City fell in 1939 from 35 percent to less than 10 percent. Babies were still prohibited from rooming in with their mothers, however. Only when Ann Campion Stewart, the obstetrical supervisor at St. Vincent's Hospital in New York City, suggested that babies and their mothers shouldn't be separated were babies finally able to sleep in their mothers' rooms rather than being left to cry alone in a nursery. Nurse Stewart recognized that babies needed hugging, kissing, and cuddling to survive and to thrive. Still, keeping mothers and their infants together did not become common practice until the 1960s.

Premature infants without the ability to regulate their own temperatures have routinely been placed in temperature-regulated glass box cribs called *isolettes*. What medical professionals have discovered, however, is that technology alone does not help these infants to thrive. Poor hospitals in Colombia, South America, did not have enough isolettes. Instead, they placed "preemies" skin to skin between their mothers' breasts. The mothers carried these infants about inside their clothing, and a baby's temperature was naturally regulated from her mother's body temperature. These babies thrived with the help of this technique, now called "kangaroo care." These "pouch" babies grow faster, cry less, breathe easier, and go home earlier than premature infants cared for in other ways.

In our technological society of the United States, many hospitals have adapted by allowing kangaroo care only soon before the baby is ready to go home. We do encourage mothers and fathers to gently stroke their babies with one or two fingers while they are in the isolette.

TOUCH STIMULATION FOR HEALTHY GROWTH

Touch is vital to stimulation of the growth hormone. It is now widely known that children suffering from touch deprivation—such as some observed in Romanian orphanages—attain only half the normal height for their age group. Touch is equally important for the mother throughout pregnancy and during labor. A friend of mine, Jack Crimmins, wrote this poem, which I think speaks to the way mothers and babies thrive through contact:

I am the one who says prayer is touch,
You are the one who says touch is prayer.
We sing of differences
We're all together here.

HYPNOTOUCH SELF-MASSAGE FOR MOTHERS

Self-massage, by which I simply mean touching yourself in a focused, conscious way, can be beneficial for relaxation and for keeping "in touch" with the changes in your body and baby. Every mother-to-be and new mother ought to give herself a daily massage. It is a wonderful way to honor yourself and your uborn. It is a good idea to use slightly warmed sesame oil. Ayurvedic practitioners recommend cooking grade oils rather than oils purchased as massage oils because the commercially prepared massage oils often contain preservatives or other additives. Because your skin absorbs these oils, the additives can have an unhealthy effect. If you don't have oil—or if you find using it to be too much trouble—it is better to massage with just your hands than not to massage at all, even if you do it for only a few minutes.

Pregnant mother self-massage: Start with your head. Grab hold of your hair and gently pull your scalp back and forth. Move your hands to your forehead, and gently and ever so lightly move four fingers from one of your hands (whichever you prefer) from right to left and left to right, back and forth across your forehead. Do this four times.

Now move your attention to your ears. Gently put each hand by its respective ear, right hand to right ear and left hand to left ear. Slowly touch all the convolutions, curves, and surfaces of your ears and then of your face. Move your hands along your face and to your neck and your shoulders. Keep touching as you continue, from your shoulders to your arms, wrists, hands, breasts, throat, chest, and abdomen.

As you reach your abdomen, stop momentarily and just be with your uborn. As you massage or rest your fingers and hands gently on your abdomen, think of the uborn there and rest for a moment.

Continue moving your fingers and hands over your body, moving down your abdomen and around to your back and buttocks. Move your hands down to your thighs, knees, calves, shins, ankles, feet, and finally each of your toes.

BENEFITS OF A
DAILY SELF-MASSAGE

This daily massage enhances your immune system, relaxes your muscles, relieves stress, and makes you healthier mentally, emotionally, and physically. It promotes healthy circulation and a sense of connection and comfort with your body and your uborn. Through these few moments of touch, you build a bond between yourself and your uborn.

When you go into the first stage of labor, this same type of massage can be used by your support person to help you relax, or you can use parts of it on yourself. As labor progresses, it works well to have your support person massage you in between contractions while you rest. The gentle rubbing of sesame oil on your waist and abdomen, your back and buttocks, can comfort you and help you relax. Long, soft strokes down your thighs, finally ending with a massage of your feet and toes and the inner leg right above your ankle, will help you through the labor.

Stimulation and gentle touching of the nipples and breasts during labor helps to bring about uterine contractions through production and release of the hormone oxytocin, which is a natural pitocin. In addition to helping the uterus contract, this hormone from the pituitary stimulates production of milk. Touching or kissing the nipples is a much healthier, safer, and more pleasant way to help the uterus contract and the body produce milk than a pitocin intravenous drip.

WHEN NOT TO TOUCH

Although touch is very important during pregnancy and labor, it is also crucial to know when not to touch. During transition, mothers usually do not like to be rubbed or stroked during contractions. This is the time when even a gentle rub can be an irritant. The best touch during transition is the ankle technique. During the ankle technique, described in detail on page 146, your support person squeezes your leg just above your left ankle simultaneously with your contraction. As your abdomen rises and the contraction becomes more intense and effective, so will the squeezing. Focus on the hand as a support on your ankle, grounding you. Because the body is unable to experience two discomforts at the same time, you will not be aware of the possible discomfort of the contraction. At this time, it is also imperative that you relax your jaw and relax your hands.

Once your baby arrives, massage can again help you, the mother. After delivery of the placenta, it is a good idea for your support person to give you another full, gentle oil massage, followed by a gentle sponge bath. It is important to continue this massage daily for the first few weeks postpartum. It will again bring comfort to your body, aid circulation, and help you relax during these weeks as your body readjusts.

If there is no one to give you this massage, give it to yourself. I can't stress enough the value of this simple technique for your benefit during and after pregnancy. After the birth, it will help prevent postpartum depression.

HYPNOTOUCH DURING LABOR

Following is a sample hypnotouch procedure to be performed during labor, beginning early, in the first stage. This is the time when contractions last about thirty to sixty seconds and come five to twenty minutes apart. After the mother and support person listen to her labor tape together, the mother sits in a chair, and the support person moves his hands symmetrically about one to two inches over the energy field of the mother's body, never actually touching her skin, which may be hypersensitive. Following are guidelines for the support person.

Begin at the head, and go down the spine and across the shoulders and back and down the legs to the feet as you move your hands in an arc. Silently observe the symmetry or asymmetry, temperature, flow of energy or stagnation, or any other sensation.

Move around to the front of the body again, beginning with the head. Move down the face, neck, shoulders, arms, hands, breasts, abdomen. Be aware of the energy of the body and move down the legs to the feet, without actually touching the skin. This initial movement is an assessment. If you feel a stagnation or an intuition about an area, work on it by helping the energy to flow freely.

During this stage of labor, movement is important: walking, rocking in a chair, alternately walking and squatting (which facilitates the opening of the pelvis and encourages the descent and rotation of the baby into the proper birthing position).

This is a good time to put on some prechosen slow dance music and do hypnotouch while dancing. As you dance and touch, use your intention to send loving, relaxation, and compassion to each other. At this time, you can speak to each of the parts as you actually touch them, letting your words flow with your own healing intuition for the purpose always of helping the mother to relax and center and remain open and conscious to her birthing process.

As the contractions become more intense, if the mother's membranes are still intact, she could take a soothing bath while the support person does hypnotouch with warm sesame oil, starting at the scalp and working down her body with long, downward strokes, or, while the mother showers she could sit on a stool. While she is sitting, the support person can wash the oil from her hair and massage her belly, hips, thighs, legs, and feet with warm sesame oil. This helps to open up the pelvis and is extremely relaxing.

Once the contractions are five minutes apart on a regular basis, it is a good idea to be at your birthing site. Continue to apply the oil to the belly with gentle, circular motions. Apply oil to the legs, hips, and feet, with gentle, yet firm, long strokes.

During transition, the cervix dilates from eight to ten centimeters, and contractions occur frequently. The touch to use during this phase is the ankle-squeezing technique. This is the period when sounding—such as chanting or repeating the vowel sounds, "aaaaaaaaaa," "eeeeeeeeeeee," "iiiiiiiiiiiiiiiiii," "oooooooooooo," "uuuuuuuuuuuuu," ending each with the "um" sound, aum, cum, ium, oum, uum—is most effective and necessary. (You can learn more about this in Chapter Nine.) This is the period when touch, except for the ankle-squeezing technique, should be in the energy field only. The mother's skin should not be disturbed during this time. Touching can be an irritant and make her tense rather than relaxed.

Here's how this phase might transpire. Contraction is occurring. The support person is squeezing the ankle gently, gradually increasing the intensity of squeezing pressure as the contraction rises. As the ankle is being squeezed, the support person is using a hypnotic voice, with a slow, steady beat, saying, "Relax your jaw. Relax your hands. Ah, eee, iii, o, u. Focus on my hand, which is on your left ankle. Wonderful. You're doing very well. Your concentration is right there. Good work."

As the support person, you should pause often, never with a barrage of words. Speak a sentence and then an observation, and send your loving and compassionate energy silently. Then say another encouraging phrase. Right now, during this phase, the most important thing is for the support person to remember this mantra: "Relax your jaw. Relax your hands. Focus on my hand on your left ankle." The support person should repeat this at the beginning of each contraction.

Between contractions, there should be silence, with the mother resting. The support person should place both hands gently and firmly and *still* on the mother's feet. Sit quietly, patiently, and compassionately, while all the time sending concentrated energy to easily, readily help the flow of the mother's energy to allow for the easy passage of the baby down and out of the birth canal.

Ankle-squeezing technique: When the contractions are most intense, the support person puts his hand very firmly around the mother's left ankle and squeezes. Rather than focusing on the contractions, the mother focuses on this squeeze and imagines a healing white light flowing from the squeezing hand into and around her ankle. Our bodies cannot really feel more than one sensation at once. By focusing on this squeeze, you will not be aware of other sensations (such as the contractions) in your body. You will be aware of the intensity of the white light in your ankle.

For most of you, indulging in sensual and fulfilling touching was how the uborn got started in the first place. Use these touch techniques to increase intimacy and stay connected to each other during pregnancy and once the baby arrives.

Chapter Nine

A MUSICAL FEAST

THE MAGIC OF SOUND

The life of your baby depends on the proper rhythmical functioning of your body and your baby's body and the syn-
chronicity of the two. Both bodies are pulled along at your pace,
breathing and receiving nourishment and resting when you do
those things. They become a part and are influenced by each of
your body's motions and functions. Your uborn becomes entrained
to your rhythm, no matter what it is.

All of life is a swell of rhythms and the vibrations accompanying those rhythms. Health is the perfect balance of all internal
rhythms and can be enhanced by the proper external ones.

Sound, both audible and inaudible, surrounds and consti-
tutes all of life. Each sound has a pitch that resonates either bene-
ficially or restrictively to the human organism. Certain sounds
are exalting. It is those sounds that we are interested in for the
proper growth and development of the uborn and the developing
mind/body of the child.

While you are carrying your uborn in utero, she absorbs all of your experiences. While growing inside of you, your uborn experiences the vibrations and music of your body: the air moving through your lungs; the digestive rumblings in your intestines; the rhythmic and beautiful beating of your heart; the fluids released through your bladder; your swallowing, humming, gargling, singing, laughing, and talking. Each of these sounds becomes the music of the uborn's life. One of the most powerful and beneficial impressions that you can use to uplift your uborn in the healthy development of her mind, body, spirit, and intuitive faculties is the realm and wonder and splendor of music.

Scientists now know that a drug is most effective when a specific receptor exists for the drug. The receptor is a molecule outside the cell that initiates a cellular response from that drug. No drug can initiate a cellular response more readily than the harmony of music. It seems that our entire being, all the pathways in our bodies, are activated when exposed to music. In research monitoring the uborn's movements in response to various stimulants, including sound, touch, and pressure, the response to vibrations was the most powerful.

HOW SOUND AFFECTS US

Stop for a moment and listen to the most distant sounds you can hear, then to the closer ones. Is there exaltation of birds anywhere, or a brushing of branches, a flowing of waters? Move in a bit closer to the sounds of your own heart. How do each of these sounds make you feel? Your baby is the expression of your genes, his father's genes, and your internal music. Your entire body is charged with sounds that either attract or repel your baby. Many researchers believe that the intrauterine environment affects how genes are expressed.[1] In other words, the old puzzle about nature

---

1. Alessandra Piontelli, *From Fetus to Child* (London: Routledge, 1992), and Thomas Verny, *The Secret Life of the Unborn Child* (New York: Dell Publishing, 1981).

versus nurture is difficult to solve, even before the baby is born. Can music enhance the channel communications between cells? If so, would this influence the stabilization and proper functioning of the genes? Can certain musical rhythms protect the proper functioning of our cells?

Music is merely rhythmic pulses of different wavelengths. Some rhythms have been found to be more healing to the cells; others have proven to be harmful. The enjoyment of music does not necessarily mean that it is beneficial to the cells. Teenagers who enjoy listening endlessly to rock music can still lose their hearing, and that hearing loss is related to the vibrational frequency of the music that creates the volume.

According to quantum mechanics, the body is basically made up of wave vibrations. Music consists of wave vibrations of sound and therefore has varied effects on the body. Music can change blood pressure and pulse rate, for example. It can alter metabolism and the rates of heartbeat and respiration. Research has shown that music affects gastric motility, dilation of the pupils, muscle contraction (and the uterus is a muscle), and the electrical conductivity of the skin. At the University of Kansas Medical Center in Kansas City, music is used in the labor and birthing rooms. The presence of music there has routinely decreased the need for anesthesia and shortened the period of labor.

HEALING VIBRATIONS

The changes in the body previously mentioned can easily be observed, but music can also have an effect at the cellular level. Research studies have demonstrated that different musical vibrations have different effects, including the alteration of neurochemicals and hormones in the body. In one study, five types of cancer cells were subject to various types of sound and music and their growth rates recorded. Soft chanting sounds and hard rock music were two of the sounds used. Soft chanting significantly decreased the growth in all types of cancer cells studied, and hard rock music increased the growth.

It isn't hard to imagine that the cells forming in your uborn's body are equally as sensitive to sounds. When we respond to the vibrations of healing sounds, we feel more open and full, joyous and harmonious—and research is showing that this response is mirrored in our cells. The very particles of our bodies respond to and can be healed by sounds.

In many Eastern traditions, there is more respect not only for the uplifting aspect of music but also for the scientific aspects. Followers of these traditions believe that certain strains of music should be played at certain seasons; other strains are to be played at certain times of the day or night. This attitude was not just a passing fancy. Classical Hindu music has specific *ragas*, or compositions, for different hours of the day, for example. Traditionalists believe that frequencies are different at different times of the day and that the body constantly responds to these shifts in nature. The ragas are designed to help the body gracefully adapt to these subtle shifts throughout the morning, afternoon, evening, and night. When used out of their designated time frame, these compositions are not so appealing.

Just as there is an hour for certain music, there is also an aspect of music that brings out an inclination to dance or sing or maintain a state of repose. Think of music that seems appropriate for an early morning when you are trying to get children off to school in a calm manner. I doubt that you would choose hard rock or rap music. A romantic candlelit dinner would require a different type of music, and reggae might be just the thing to get you moving if you find yourself in a midafternoon slump.

The natural rhythm of the mother is expressed through her pulsation and heartbeats, through her inhalations and exhalations. It is expressed in her walking strides or gait, her direction (straight ahead or in circles), her fingers still or pleasantly occupied or tapping. It is expressed by her feet, grounded and still or with restless leg syndrome. All of these rhythms are a result of your mind and at the same time have an effect on your mind.

We find certain sounds irritating and nerve wracking and others calming and soothing. Some sounds make us angry, sad, or nostalgic. Others help us to be present in the now and to feel a clarity of mind, body, and spirit.

The musical arrangement of rhythms is an expression of mathematics. When the rhythm of a human being is discordant, she becomes irritable and restless and has a need to satisfy a longing, a longing that is deep in her nature.

CREATING BABY WITH MUSIC

The first teacher the baby has is you, his mother. If you create the proper environment for your baby, he will eventually be able to learn all that is necessary for him to fulfill his nature. All learning requires concentration, however. Many people in our society have a disturbed sense of concentration and incoherent cell rhythms.

Music is the simplest way to develop concentration, tenderness, patience, and calm. The gentle beginnings of life in utero thrive on the regular rhythm of your heart, the flow of your blood, and the correct mathematical vibration of music. Playing proper, well-chosen music for yourself, your family, and your developing uborn can have amazing manifestations for the rest of your lives.

Is your baby the visible form of the sounds it experienced while in utero? Probably. Every word has an effect on the mother; every sound has an effect on her metabolism and the rhythm of her heart and the circulation of her oxygen in her blood and the firing of her nerves. Try not to accept this chapter in theory only. Give yourself permission to experience the benefits of particular sounds and experiment with them.

The health of you, the mother, and the healthy growth and development of your uborn come about when you are both in a condition of perfect tone and rhythm. A simple way to put you and your baby in order is to play music that is in order. The *Leclaire Smart Beginnings Music* tape that we have developed for you and your baby is one of the outward treatments to create and maintain your inward balance, order, and harmony. All of the exercises and treatments offered in this book are a part of the prescription for creating the perfect health and development of you and your baby.

Let your baby be an outcome of the harmony of your nine glorious months. Allow music to fill your pregnancy, to vibrate every atom of your baby's being. I have found that babies prefer Baroque music, and Sheila Ostrander, Lynn Schroeder, and Nancy Ostrander, in their book *Superlearning*,[2] help to explain why. They discuss the commonalities between the vibration in sound, color, the bonds of chemicals, and the vibrations of electrons in an atom. They describe Baroque music as being rich in higher frequencies. Because of these higher frequencies, internationally recognized Dr. Alfred Tomatis chose to use Baroque music in the treatment of dyslexic children. Dr. Tomatis used sound therapy and developed a Baroque music method of learning for these children that was eventually adapted for language training. The largo, or slow, movements of Baroque music were used because of the slow, restful tempo of forty to sixty beats per minute. The psychophysical effects of this music create a relaxed concentration.

I have followed the suggestions presented in *Superlearning* and have used this music with cancer patients, pregnant mothers, and newborn infants for many years. The same music that can help in the learning of academic facts can also help relieve the perception of contractions. Mothers who use Baroque music during labor and later during breastfeeding have an amazingly effective relaxation response. Labor is shortened, and breastfeed-

2. Sheila Ostrander et al., *Superlearning* (New York: Delacorte Press, 1982).

ing becomes a time of calm and bonding, with the milk flowing freely. When the baby becomes irritable or bored, playing this music seems to engage and calm him almost instantly.

A few years ago, I was on a seemingly endless flight to Israel. I had with me a cassette player and a Baroque music tape. We were many hours into the flight, and everyone around me was restless and fidgeting. It seemed the entire plane was walking about. In the midst of this *passagiata*, a child of about three years began to scream uncontrollably. The sound was painful, and I could almost feel the deep distress of the baby.

After about fifteen minutes of the child's nonstop screaming, somehow many of us had found out the apparent cause. Her very patient mother said the little girl was autistic and had been given a medication to relax her during the long flight. The drug seemingly had a paradoxical effect.

With nothing to lose, the mother agreed to try the music. There were no speakers on the player; the sound came through the earphones. This presented a problem, but we devised a listening method. The mother sat in one seat and held her child while I sat next to her and held the earphones near the child. In six to eight minutes, the girl's anguished wailing subsided, and shortly thereafter she fell asleep.

MAGICAL, MUSICAL REST

Rest now for twenty minutes and play your *Leclaire Smart Beginnings Music* tape. Enjoy the experience of the music as you rise above thought, as you transcend form, as you give your uborn peaceful amniotic floatings.

The amniotic fluid absorbs much of the sound but does not filter the cadence, tone, volume, and stress. When newborns hear the calming music that was repeatedly played for them before birth, they become attentively relaxed and very interested. They respond differently postpartum to sounds they have heard prenatally.

To try to teach your uborn vocabulary in the uterus, you have to expose him to very loud volumes in order to bring the words and phrases clearly to the womb. This can be harmful. I believe that it is also an unreasonable burden to place on your uborn. This is a time for him to grow and gently develop, not to learn language skills.

The first rule of medicine is "do no harm." Baroque music does no harm, and it helps the uborn while away her days in utero and molds the neural circuits in a healthy fashion. The meaning of the sounds is created by the sounds themselves. *Leclaire Smart Beginnings Music* means relaxation and calm, uplift for mother. Compounded with the sound of music the uborn hears, this creates an eternal response to music thus associated with being nurtured and soothed. Later on, after birth, the baby will enjoy bonding with the mother while the same music is being played. It creates a cellular memory for both. This is a good time for the mother to talk with the uborn as he picks up on the calm and centered and soothing tone of the mother's voice. Because the uborn is able to sense the emotional tone and level of stress in your voice, it is important to set a time to talk when you are soothed, relaxed, and tranquil. This exciting knowledge allows you to truly bring peace to the world one baby at a time.

Dr. Thomas Verny, in his book *The Secret Life of the Unborn Child*, tells the story of Boris Brott, a conductor who told of his engagement with music since he was a uborn. His mother was a cellist, and while carrying Boris she practiced certain pieces over and over. When Brott had to conduct certain scores for the first time, he would already know the cello line; he would know the flow of the music even before he turned the page of the score or saw the line written. One day he mentioned this phenomenon to his mother. When he told her the musical pieces, she said they were the ones she had practiced over and over when she was pregnant.

Another mother I know was a French horn player. During her first pregnancy, she was preparing to audition for a job in a prestigious symphony orchestra. She rehearsed over and over, working out small details of each piece that would be part of her audition repertory. Once her son was born, she no longer needed to rehearse as much, but she was working on concert music. Her boy slept fitfully and often cried from colic. She had trouble practicing her instrument while he was awake because he needed attention. She didn't want to practice while he slept for fear the loud tones of the French horn would wake him.

One day, at his naptime, she needed to practice a particularly difficult part before a concert that was fast approaching. Her son cried, not wanting to go down for his nap. Rocking him didn't help; walking with him didn't help; soothing him in his crib didn't help. Finally, in frustration, she put him in the crib, still crying, and decided to practice anyway, cries or no cries. To her surprise, while she was warming up on a few scales, playing in the same room with him to keep an eye on him, he settled in and fell fast asleep. At that moment she realized that although he could not "hear" her practicing through the nine months she carried him, he had become accustomed to the vibrations of the music. From then on, she used his naptime to play in another room, knowing that the muffled sounds of her scales and exercises would bring him restful sleep.

CREATING YOUR OWN MUSICAL SOUNDS

Many women have found great comfort in chanting their own mantras during pregnancy (or anytime, really). Many religious traditions use chanting to induce a trance state or simply to sing praises or say prayers. The prayers commonly used with the rosary in the Roman Catholic Church might be considered mantras, for example. Catholics repeat these mantras while keeping track of how many times they are said. Gregorian chants have been recorded in cathedrals around the world, and the sound is relaxing and empowering.

In the section on labor and birth (see page 146), I suggest a mantra that fathers can use to calm the mother and to help her remember the things she should do to remain calm and focused. You can create your own mantra, based on the things you most want to remember to do, or use prayers you already know. In meditation classes, I have learned these simple mantras, and even though I did not understand the language I used at first, they have proven effective to help me enter a state of peace and to quiet the mind.

- Hebrew mantra: "Yod hey vav hey." This is actually the spelling of the name of God, Yahweh, in Hebrew.
- Christian mantra: "Ma ra na tha." This means "come, Lord" in Aramaic.
- Buddhist mantra: "Nam mo a di da phat." This is calling the name of the Buddha.
- Nonreligious mantra: "Pa cem ma." This means "peace" in Latin (plus an extra syllable—ma—for fluidity.)

Try one or several of these mantras in your meditation practice. They can sound like music, and they can become a signal to your body to enter the meditative state.

Sound to Soothe or Energize

We now know that sound has an immediate effect on the frequency of the brain waves, including those of a developing child. I was once at a one-week retreat, working with cancer patients, when all the staff and patients had the wonderful opportunity to work with a group of Native Indians. An elder of the group uses different drum rhythms to create different states of consciousness. At the ceremony, the elder was to play one drum, and I was given another. Everyone else in the room was to go on a visualization trip into the depths of Earth through an imaginary hole in the ground, while my role was to follow the beat and play it along with the lead drummer.

My one disappointment before the ceremony was that I couldn't just let go and get into a trance like the rest of the group of "visualizers." I considered it neither a privilege nor an honor to be the one awake and beating the drum. I felt as though I were still working instead of playing, and I wanted the drumming to begin.

Most people reclined on the carpeted floor of the conference room; some sat in chairs with their eyes closed. Earlier in the day, we had been asked to collect certain objects from nature, such as feathers and stones, to be used as part of the ritual, acknowledged as part of the sacred journey.

The slow, rhythmic drumming began, and I slowly followed the lead drummer as well as his guided imagery. I began to feel as though the drum and I had been together for all time, and rather than impeding my guided journey, I believe, it enhanced it. I didn't even realize that I was in a trance. I lost my observing ego and apparently was completely in the present. When the lead drummer brought us out with three authoritative beats and I followed with the same, I realized I had truly been in the most magnificent trance I had ever had in meditation.

It felt most restorative. The patients and the other staff all agreed that it stimulated something deep in their body and psyche. This is what healing is about. It is generated from within rather than from without, unlike the usual treatments used in traditional Western, allopathic medicine, which are external. Music and sound, although originating from outside, affect the entire mind/body, creating specific responses, either balancing or unbalancing in the system depending on the sound vibration and frequency.

THE HEALING POWER OF HYPNOACOUSTICS

I have created a new term to describe the effects of music on the mental, spiritual, and physical health of both mother and baby. This term, *hypnoacoustics,* means the intentional use of voice, sound, and music to stimulate the body's natural healing mechanisms. I have experienced these effects myself for many years, and I have found many ways in which we use music and sound for these purposes, whether consciously or otherwise.

My interest in the healing power of music and sound began in my grandmother's arms. No matter what needed healing, all she had to do was to begin her soft Italian chant, "Oh, Mother, how pretty the moon is tonight. It was never so pretty before." Immediately I was in a trance.

Music and healing are inseparable for me. I spent much time in my early years listening to the healing music of Gregorian chant and opera. In the Catholic church where I attended daily mass with either my mother or grandfather, I was routinely hypnotized by the singsong voice of the priest reciting the liturgy in Latin. Later, in my adolescence, Elvis Presley, calypso, and the Platters took over. In my young adulthood, nothing healed me like all the great sounds of jazz, Bach, Handel, and Vivaldi.

The goal of healing music is to address all the frequencies of the brain and to move the frequencies downward to a state of healing. These different states of the brain are measured as electrical frequencies and are in fact nothing more than cycles per second (called hertz). The frequencies are *beta,* the normal working and active state; *alpha,* the state of daydreaming and imagery; *theta,* the deep meditative state; and *delta,* a deep reparative sleep state.

These frequencies can be measured with an electroencephalogram. In hypnoacoustics, however, certain sounds, particular tones of voice, and specific healing words and music are used to consciously and intentionally manipulate the brainwaves. I developed hypnoacoustics specifically for pregnancy, labor, and birthing, but it can be used for all healing. I have also used it with cancer patients and for chronic pain.

Case Study: Grace

One expectant mother, Grace, was so agitated when she came to see me that she could barely sit down; she would actually pace back and forth. Grace was six months pregnant and had begun to have severe anxiety attacks every time she thought about giving birth. She was terrified of a vaginal birth and even more terrified of a cesarean section. She was actually in one of the most agitated states I have ever seen anyone who was not psychotic.

About six months prior to my meeting with Grace, I had been shopping with a friend when we had come upon a rainstick—a cylinder three inches in diameter and filled with tiny pebbles. When the rainstick is inverted, the most beautiful rainlike sounds are released as the pebbles gradually or rapidly fall through the cylinder. The effect changes with the angle at which the rainstick is held.

The rainstick was made of a gorgeous light wood, and I fell in love with it. My friend just laughed, thinking how absurd it would be to use it with all of my usual left brain clients, such as lawyers, physicians, accountants, and professors. I had brought it to my office, but I never used it until one day when I was pacing back and forth with Grace. Talking gently and softly, I gradually slowed my pace to a hypnotic, trance-like walk, hoping she would do the same. I suddenly had an intuition. I asked if she would be willing to try something. In a previous session she had refused to listen to music. She agreed this time.

Grace sat in the chair, and eventually she rested on her left side on a mat on the floor. As I continued to speak quietly with her, I began to move the rainstick around and about her body, letting the pebbles ever so slowly drop to the bottom. I could see her relax. Her eyes closed, and her eye movements, which I could see under her eyelids, slackened; her jaw was no longer clenched, and her hands were relaxed. After a few weeks she began to believe that she could give birth to her baby, either vaginally or with a cesarean section.

We worked like this once a week for about ten weeks. Before this, when I had asked her to rank her anxiety from one to ten, she had described it as thirty; she said it was off the scale, and she didn't want to give it a number. By the time she gave birth, she was describing it as a four. She planned to have a heavily medicated, noninduced vaginal birth, with as large an episiotomy as her doctor wanted to give her.

In the end Grace didn't need as much medication as she was willing to take. The healing sound of the rainstick had certainly altered Grace's brainwaves in such a way that she could visualize or perceive a normal vaginal birth, and eventually she did give birth vaginally to her son, Ben.

Chapter Ten

TOWARD LIBERATION
OF BIRTH

SETTING ATTAINABLE GOALS

An actor prepares and studies and prepares and rehearses and prepares and tries out for each role he undertakes. A musician prepares and studies and prepares and rehearses for each performance she gives. A writer rewrites and revises and researches. Every occupation I can think of demands attention and preparation, yet many women don't take any time to learn about their body and the processes of pregnancy and labor before they give birth. Preparation will help you to understand the changes taking place in your body. It will teach you about the growth of your new baby. Perhaps, most important of all, preparation will make labor a familiar and easy procedure for you.

Any experience can be frightening if you haven't had it before or if you don't know what to expect. Think of your first day of school. Perhaps you felt anxiety. By the end of the first week, though, you had new friends, and you liked your teacher. You looked forward to going back on Monday morning. What about the first time you drove a car? Were you afraid? Now you probably climb into the car without a second thought. When you try anything for the first time, you must first understand what you want to accomplish. You must understand your goals and then set about reaching for them in small steps. The first time you drove, you probably took every step slowly: put the key in the ignition; fasten the seatbelt; check the mirrors; start the engine. You probably drove around a parking lot or a deserted street. Now you don't think about those steps, and you drive on the freeway without hesitation. Perhaps you're not ready to drive a racecar, but you can negotiate your city with very little conscious thought.

Pregnancy, birth, and labor can seem just as natural to you if you learn what is happening in your body and take easy steps. This chapter helps you to set easy, attainable goals that will help you become familiar with the process of bringing your baby into the world.

EXPLODING THE MYTHS OF LABOR

The first step of any process is learning what to expect. Many myths surround childbirth, and our society has accepted as fact many of these myths, such as that labor must be a torturous experience. Pavlov taught us that even the most pleasant of associations can be conditioned to become fear provoking if paired with an unpleasant or frightening stimulus.

The story of Sarah (see Chapter One) illustrates this concept particularly well. Sarah had to wait after work for her husband in a bad neighborhood each night, and then she often fought with him. Although getting off of work, going home to dinner, and relaxing are pleasant associations for most people, Sarah associated arguing with her husband with this period of time. Instead of looking forward to the end of her workday, she dreaded it.

In Western society, childbirth has often been paired with horror stories of pain, puerperal fever, even death. This exaggeration of fear around childbirth and the role of the father as a bumbling idiot have been perpetuated by the movie and entertainment industry. Such film footage may be dramatic and can produce laughs and tears, but it helps to perpetuate the following myths in our culture:

- Childbirth is painful and unbearable. I have heard many firsthand stories from friends and relatives. I have seen the agony of the mother innumerable times on the movie screen.
- Labor inevitably ends up as a stressful emergency. I have often seen a screaming, out-of-control woman rushed on a stretcher through the corridors of a hospital to a delivery room (not a birthing room).
- The mother, now in agony, finds it impossible to birth her baby. It becomes imperative for the doctor to put her out of her misery and to subsequently deliver the baby for her.
- The father remains helpless and ridiculous, a buffoon of sorts, adding the necessary comic relief to the drama at hand.

Just as good education should bring us back to our original essence, so should good culture elevate our basic natures. Western culture seems to have adversely affected the natural function of our birthing. It has taken a relatively painless event, a beautiful miracle of life, and turned it into a period of anxiety, exhaustion, fear, and pain. We need to reclaim the joy, as well as the natural ability, that is our heritage as women. By embracing the process, we can experience birth in this better way, combining the joy of the women of Our Lady of Angels parish with the knowledge we now share about the connection between our minds and bodies. We must take back the birthing process, allowing the joy, focus, and excitement of pregnancy, labor, and birthing to return to our lives. This is our right of passage.

CHILDBIRTH THROUGH EARLY HISTORY

A second grader, when asked the definition of history, said it is something that goes on and on and on. The history of childbirth in European civilization has fostered the concept of pain and suffering as essential components. It is possible to stop this artificial idea of childbirth by reconnecting ourselves to the beauty and simplicity of childbirth that "indigenous" (natural) women have experienced for all time. These women expect an easy and unlabored childbirth, and that is what they experience. They are in accord with their own unaffected nature.

Relaxed childbirth conforms to the laws of nature. Hippocrates (about 400 B.C.), the father of medicine, stressed prevention of complications through discipline in diet, exercise, and fresh air. He also concentrated on self-healing through attending to our own nature. He taught his students not to interfere with nature, to intervene only in case of emergency, to first do no harm, and to not administer any deadly drugs.

Aristotle (384–322 B.C.) recognized that the mind of the mother must be cared for during pregnancy. Soranus, the grand authority of obstetrics in Greece, wrote a treatise in A.D. 79 on obstetrics in which he emphasized acknowledging the "women's feelings." Fear was not a normal occurrence during childbirth at that time.

During the sixteenth century, women continued to birth with midwives, sometimes called *good mothers* or *wise women,* just as they had always done. At that time, however, physicians—who were called in only when the situation was desperate—began to keep written accounts of the births they attended. Then, in the seventeenth century, physicians dismissed and rejected many age-old practices of medicine as superstition. These physicians (at that time men) began to impose their own ways of perceiving pregnancy. They believed that any fright of the mother—seeing a thing, hearing a story, experiencing a frightful animal or person— would have a rebound on the being of the child. Women were encouraged to remove themselves from society to avoid these traumas.

Recognizing the influence a happy mother had on a healthy infant, experts during the eighteenth century recommended a lighthearted approach to pregnancy. According to Jacques Gelis's *History of Childbirth: Fertility, Pregnancy, and Birth in Early, Modern Europe*, it became "common to see children stained from birth with a thousand defects they have brought from the womb of a dejected, quick tempered, capricious, or intemperate mother. Vices were seen as infections, like diseases. An expectant mother must be lighthearted, she should be merry and gay. But this does not depend on her alone. A good environment also helps to make a good pregnancy."

During these centuries, women in labor still listened to their own bodies, thus intuitively choosing positions that helped them to birth comfortably and quickly. The positions of choice were sitting, squatting, kneeling, being on all fours, and standing. Women also naturally changed positions throughout their labor to reduce fatigue and to stimulate the contractions and help the baby descend through the birth canal. Until the nineteenth century, fathers were allowed in the birthing room only when their strength was needed to support the mother during a hard labor.

After the seventeenth-century advent of the new birthing chair, similar to ancient Greek chairs, fathers were no longer necessary. The birthing chair, designed by a man, restricted the mother's movement during her labor. Thus it became a symbol to her of physical pain.

CHILDBIRTH IN THE TWENTIETH CENTURY

The twentieth century brought new language to birth. Women stopped "giving birth" and were "delivered." Physicians, now in charge of births, condemned the various positions a woman naturally chose as indecent, repellent, and animal like. Mothers were put on their backs, in a supine position. This position, chosen by the medical men, was the worst possible position for the mother. Now the pain of childbirth became severe; labor could not progress naturally in this position. Compression of the inferior vena cava occurred, thus causing fetal distress. This position also became a factor in severely decreasing the mother's blood pressure.

New medications came into play to "help" the mother do what women had done successfully, and with less severe pain, for millennia. Use of anesthesia and analgesia, however, caused prolongation of the second stage of labor, inhibited voluntary cooperation of the mother, and enhanced the use of forceps. Forceps were used to draw the baby out during difficult or problem deliveries and therefore shortened the length of delivery. They became common tools to speed up the process. Forceps delivery gave way to an increase in cesarean sections.

In 1933, British physician Grantly Dick Read recognized a need to help pregnant and laboring women reduce their fear surrounding childbirth. He believed in abolishing the physiological climate (created by the medical profession) that creates and worsens pain. He respected women's intuition and spiritual knowledge. Read advocated helping the mother abandon her fear by enlightening her to her physical and psychological changes and spiritual needs. He was unable to work out a coherent method of positive application of his Natural Childbirth Methods, however.

In 1949, Elizabeth Bing, later to become cofounder of Lamaze International, began training women in Dr. Read's techniques; in 1951 she began educating women in New York. She taught them about labor and relaxation and continued Dr. Read's work as outlined in a handbook written by Helen Heardman. Altered chest breathing as a technique for relaxation and other relaxation techniques become part of her regular childbirth classes.

Then, in 1956, Fernand Lamaze, M.D., observed techniques of the Russian medical system and founded the concept of Painless Childbirth. He disagreed with Dr. Read on the spiritual and intuitive aspects of pregnancy and labor, believing that cognitive reorganization and the influence of consciousness could help a woman deliver a child herself without pain. Dr. Lamaze added mind/body medicine long before it was acceptable in the medical community. He felt that the most important preparation for childbirth was the psychological preparation of the mother. To reach a complete solution to the problems arising from previous perceptions of childbirth, we first had to abolish the belief that pain is a natural concomitant of childbirth. This belief is still an integral part of our society. The name Lamaze has become synonymous with general childbirth classes.

Meanwhile, Robert H. Bradley, M.D., had met with Dr. Read in 1948 to discuss Dr. Read's theories, and in 1962 Bradley published a paper that encouraged fathers to participate in birth, effectively putting the father in charge of "managing" the labor and delivery.[1] In the midst of Dr. Lamaze's and Dr. Read's work, Dr. Bradley introduced Natural Childbirth the Bradley Way in 1984. Classes advocating his methods concentrated on relaxation as the key to a successful labor. All drugs were considered bad during pregnancy and were discouraged. This technique ignored the emotional aspects of the mother and her relationship to the real world of obstetrical birth and alienated the medical community, however. Bradley lay teachers often disparaged nurses, nurse midwives, and physicians as poor teachers.

---

1. "Father's Presence in the Delivery Room," in *Psychosomatics* 6, no. 3.

Even with these new methods, women were not in control of births. By 1987, one out of four babies born in the United States was by cesarean section, and many of these seemed more a matter of convenience than of medical necessity. The prime time for cesarean sections, for example, was before 5:30 P.M.—before dinnertime for the doctors. Before major holidays, such as Christmas, New Year's, and Thanksgiving, the percentage of cesarean sections for some doctors soared to 75 percent. In Brazil, cesarean sections became the preferred method of delivery among the wealthy society women and accounted for 90 percent of the clinic births in the country. By contrast, midwives such as Ina May Gaskin continued to help women give birth without intervention. At Gaskin's Midwifery Farm in Tennessee during the late 1980s, the cesarean section rate was 1.5 percent after 1,700 births.

In 1988, the American College of Obstetricians and Gynecologists advocated abandoning the medical tenet that once a cesarean section is performed, the woman must give birth by cesarean section from then on. For the first time, women with previous cesarean section births had the option of vaginal delivery.

The medical establishment continues to control births and birthing. A lay midwife was arrested at gunpoint in her home by the California Board of Medical Quality Assurance in 1990. Her three children looked on as she was taken into custody for operating a school for lay midwives. In 1991, a lay midwife in northern California was arrested for practicing nursing and medicine without a license while teaching a breastfeeding class. The quality of attention to a woman's options has declined, and the mothers and babies suffer. Although women have more choices in many aspects of their lives than ever, they are often still at the mercy of huge medical conglomerates when it comes to birthing babies. They are not always offered the choices they need or informed of the options they have to birth their babies.

This brief glance at the history of childbirth as it developed from being woman centered to being physician centered over the centuries may prove enlightening. It may help you to understand why the Leclaire Method is necessary. Today we might say it is normal and usual for a woman to feel fear surrounding childbirth. To again see pregnancy and childbirth as a harmonious and natural time, we must reclaim it and overcome the obstacles of fear put into our path through our culture. The Leclaire Method with Hypnosis will help you take charge of your pregnancy while guiding you to seek any assistance you need.

NATURAL MIND/BODY PREGNANCY FOR TODAY'S MOTHERS

When Dr. Lamaze first observed Soviet women giving birth, he was amazed at the outcome. Between 86 and 92 percent of the women with vaginal births gave birth without pain. Later, the Soviet methods Lamaze had observed were used in China with the same results. The general belief of the Russian health team, Lamaze, and Read was that pain and fear in pregnancy and childbirth were a tradition, a social phenomenon. This phenomenon needed to be exploded so that pain and fear could be looked upon as useless.

When I began working with pregnant women in 1987, I believed that pain was a message to the body. I wondered why women had pain in childbirth. Was it only a social phenomenon? I thought about women of long ago, planting and gathering their food. Perhaps pain as an accompaniment to contractions was a message to her that she should leave the field and get close to home so that she could rest and conserve energy for the work of birth. If she needed this initial warning, however, it would seem to me that now that she was safe and knew she had begun labor, the message was no longer necessary. Other normal bodily functions are not painful—for example, defecation, urination, breathing, ejaculation, orgasm. Some women even speak of experiencing an orgasm during birth. I have worked with people with chronic pain, and I have observed the pain diminish as social support, relaxation, and purpose in life increase. So I began to think deeply about Lamaze's and Read's belief and decided to explore these ideas further. This is how the Leclaire Method came to be.

The first law of medicine is "do no harm." That is the goal of the Leclaire Method. This program puts neither mother nor baby at risk. Quite to the contrary. It eliminates many complications and enhances self-esteem and mother/infant bonding. Mothers recover, and the method upgrades the scene for the baby, allowing her to latch on to the breast more readily and to be more content in general.

Preparing yourself physically and psychologically for a healthy pregnancy and a relaxed and pain-free labor does not mean that you will not feel your baby proceeding through the birth canal. You will be able to feel your contractions, which I prefer to call "rhythmic risings," in a calm, relaxed manner. You may choose to ask for medication, or you may experience no need for medication. You will at least have a choice. Either way, you can be successful.

REDEFINING PREGNANCY AND LABOR

One of the ways of attacking the myths of fear and pain in childbirth is to redefine labor. Labor is usually broken down into four stages: Stage I—latent, active, and transition phases, with regular uterine contractions in the early stage; Stage II—complete cervical dilation begins and and ends with birth; Stage III—begins immediately after birth and ends with the separation and expulsion of the placenta; and Stage IV—begins after the expulsion of the placenta and extends through the first hour after childbirth.

For our purposes, we should divide labor into five stages and include the preliminary stage of labor. This stage, preceding the traditional first stage, ideally begins three months prior to conception and is the time when the mother and her partner begin to prepare themselves physically, mentally, and spiritually for pregnancy. It is during this preliminary stage that all the preparations for true labor should begin. It is now that the prevention of maternal and fetal distress and paternal isolation begins. Buying into the negative myths of childbirth affects the regulation of a mother's hormones in a negative way, which then signal to an overflow, which in turn leads to imbalance in the autonomic nervous system and the brain of the uborn.

By the second trimester, the uborn's higher brain centers are able to sense the psychological impressions of the mother's autonomic nervous system. Thus, you should remember that your baby is under the same stress you are experiencing. This is a most important awareness for fathers as well. The behavior of the father, which oftentimes becomes erratic during pregnancy, has a great influence upon the mother's feelings and behavior and thus on the baby. Both parents should work to provide the most serene atmosphere possible. No matter what questions or concerns you have, your main goal is bonding.

Many feelings arise spontaneously during pregnancy and can't be dealt with prior to their emergence. When they do arise, it is important to deal with them rather than to deny them. It has been my observation that the mother is willing to deal with most of the conflicts of pregnancy and motherhood. Oftentimes she does not get support from the father, however. He frequently seems afraid of facing even the slightest feelings and fears that emerge. He then withdraws, which triggers the mother's fear of abandonment. The father's withdrawal is often triggered by his own fear of abandonment. Now we have a vicious cycle—each afraid of being abandoned, each experiencing his or her greatest fear. What must the innocent ego of the uborn be experiencing across the neuro-hormonal pathway? How can this be resolved so that all needs are met? The solution is simple, yet not so very easy.

LIBERATION FROM FEAR AND PAIN
THROUGH YOUR OWN MIND

We should always strive to be our truest selves, and to do this we must articulate the myriad of feelings that arise as a result of pregnancy. You are not alone in these feelings. You *are* alone when you don't speak of them, however—when you isolate yourself and distance yourself from your mate.

Even so, some form of retreat can be an appropriate way to get in touch with feelings surrounding pregnancy. Taking a retreat during pregnancy can be appropriate. This should not be done in a hostile way, but in a self-searching, loving way. It is proper and fitting for the father to go off by himself in nature for three days or so, and for the mother to do the same—a time for a vision quest of sorts, a time to get in touch with one's own spirit and life force and true inner desires and needs. When we are quiet, it is easier to know what we really want and need. When we really know what we want and need, we can more readily ask directly for it or give it to ourselves. When we meet our own needs, it is easier to meet the needs of our partner and of our children. All of these emotions, thoughts, and feelings affect the onset and outcome of true labor. Thus, you can see the importance of the preparatory stage. This perhaps is the most important stage of all.

I used to teach six-week classes for pregnant women and their partners. Some educators using the Leclaire Method still do. Later, however, I decided to create a one-day pregnancy retreat for teaching the method to pregnant couples. We gather on a Saturday in a beautiful, ancient indoor healing ground that happens to have a place for seminars. The day mimics labor in that couples are in a trance for the entire day and are so relaxed that the exercises dealing with feelings just seem like one more hypnotic suggestion. They flow right into the exercises. We break in the middle of the day for a delicious and mindfully prepared ayurvedic lunch. After lunch, we continue the class and complete all the main exercises in one day.

The preparatory stage of labor is a time of listening—listening to your own inner voices, to the voices of your partner, to the messages of your baby. The baby's main path of communication is through kicking. The baby often kicks when the mother moves from one position to another. He stops kicking when he is again comfortable. Loud noises can also stimulate a baby to kick vehemently, as can fetal distress. In addition, extreme negative emotions felt by the mother can create an uncomfortable environment for the baby, which he manifests by kicking.

EXERCISE: WHAT YOUR UBORN MEANS TO YOU

1. Write out all of your reasons for wanting a child. Be as honest with yourself as you can. Write all your reasons for wanting a girl child. Write all your reasons for wanting a boy child.

2. Now separate all the reasons for having a child—boy or girl—that fall under the category of persona (that is, the personality that you want to present to the world).

3. What is your purpose in life?

4. How will having a child enhance your purpose in life?

After you and your support person have done this exercise, read your answers aloud to someone of the same sex and discuss them. Then the mother and the support person read them aloud to each other and discuss them.

One couple, for example, discussed whether the mother should continue working after the baby was born and what they would give up if she did. Another discussed their hopes for a boy or a girl and the things they envisioned for that child. "I'd prefer a boy because I think boys have more opportunities in life," one said. "I want a child because I want to extend my family into the future," the other said. "I lost my mother early, and I want to build the family life I didn't have. I want a girl because I feel I missed out on knowing my mother, and I can name the child for her." "Well, I don't want to try to raise a girl," the first responded. "Too many problems with body image and hair and clothes. Boys are easier."

PAIN AND THE
PSYCHO-NEURO-HORMONAL CONNECTION

I have observed that a woman who has worked through many of her fears and anxieties in analysis often has a recurrence of these feelings during pregnancy. The unconscious of most women seems very willing to emerge and to be integrated into the self at this time. During pregnancy, a woman's emotions are close to the surface. As irrational as they may seem, oftentimes emotions have a logic to them, and they can lead us down a path right into the window of the unconscious. Both emotions and our unconscious have a life of their own, and it is important to rein them in to our conscious awareness.

During her entire pregnancy, each woman has an opportunity to make great strides in analysis or therapy, for she now approaches her own mother instinct, or lack of it. She may also be aware of her own inner child emerging, almost as a sibling in rivalry with the child in utero. The pregnant woman needs as much nurturing now as her baby will need when she arrives. The mother now begins to realize that she is at risk of having her partner transfer his libido to another. She risks his anima being connected to his new daughter, or she risks her animus being connected to her new son.

During the first trimester of pregnancy, the mother regresses in many ways to a somewhat infantile state. You may find that you require more sleep than usual, just as your newborn will. You may become irritated by loud sounds, and certain smells and tastes will become offensive, just as the newborn infant is profoundly touched by the slightest sensory input. During pregnancy, your own need for nurture may be profound, but you will learn that you can't depend solely on others to fulfill these needs.

While getting in touch with your unconscious, it is important to realize that your uborn is a part of you but that you are only the parent of the baby; you must also remember that your baby is a separate individual who has both bonding needs and individuation needs. As you bond, always realize on some level that the ultimate goal is that the baby become an individual, separate from you. The cord is cut, fusion with the placenta is cut, and fusion with the mother is severed, only to be replaced by a new form of bonding when the newborn is placed into the mother's arms and suckles at her breast.

Early in the second trimester, the pregnant mother begins to redefine many of her relationships. Her own mother now becomes the approving or disapproving grandmother-to-be. She is often, once again, the center of her mother's attention. The real apple of her mother's eye, however, is the gift they both await. If her mother is unavailable, the pregnant mother often feels the pain of her own unresolved dependency needs. When nurturing enhances pregnancy, and when the problems that emerge are addressed in a direct and caring manner, the exhilaration of birth need not be diminished by unnecessary pain.

Preparing for a Liberated Birth

Our task, then, is to deal with our attitudes and to change them in a way that will help to facilitate a joyous and pain-free birthing. It is pointless, a waste of time, and unhealthy for us to suffer because of the emotional beliefs others have imposed upon us. If we look to indigenous (natural) women and to the animal world, we see a contradiction with our own world. In the worlds of the indigenous woman and the animal, there is no apparent pain in birthing. The look of hard work on a mother's face can be confused with an effect of pain—just as the effect of a man or a woman having an orgasm can also appear to be painful. Does that mean that it is? Fear and pain as components of childbirth have entered our field of awareness. They have become images of childbirth, a part of our reality. But we can recreate that reality by examining the experience itself and by reforming the beliefs we have about it.

The Leclaire Method recognizes that the past history of childbirth is grounded in a collective memory. Women in the past and even now have allowed dispossession of what is rightfully theirs. There is a dissent among government, medical ownership, and individual freedom.

The message has been that you must go along with the medical way, or you will be abandoned by it when you really need it. In fact, those of the medical world and pregnant women need to cooperate. Who is more entitled to take charge of birth—the hospital and physician, or the mother and midwife? The freedom of maternal expression continues to erode as the rate of cesarean section rises.

The Leclaire Method enables and facilitates a greater self-reliance. As mothers resist the medical culture and their economic and technological manifestations, they can gradually rebuild the natural birthing community and return the meaningfulness of the birthing process to themselves. The "business" of birth takes over women's culture, dictates to women's bodies, and continues to shape the culture of birth, emphasizing pain and lack of control. In fact, women can be naturally powerful and in control during pregnancy and birth. The goal of the Leclaire Method is to take back our birthing rights.

Our goal is to affect the body, thus affecting the activity of the mind, which in turn helps the body to release the desired beneficial secretions that promote balance and healing and amelioration of pain and an increase in comfort and relaxation. We know that the neural activity of the brain/mind is at one with the somatic, physiologic processes of the body. Thus the mind/body interaction of biology and thought processes and behavior and their integral communication are an empirical science and not a pie-in-the-sky dream and flaky belief, as once thought. Creating the next potentially wondrous generation through conscious, healthy pregnancy; easy labor; and joyous birth is entirely possible, and you are taking the first step toward that right this minute.

EXERCISE: CREATING A LIBERATED BIRTH PLAN

First read the following:

Pain in childbirth depends upon these things:

1. Myths

2. Incorporation of myths into one's own culture

3. Acceptance of these myths with subsequent repression

4. Adoption of a belief system to one's own disadvantage

5. Fear, anxiety, and panic

6. Interpretation of your fears, anxiety, and panic without compassion

Comfort and celebration of the life force depend upon these things:

1. Myths

2. Choosing positive myths that we want to Incorporate into our culture

3. Rejection of negative myths

4. Analytic dream work

5. Acceptance of the new and positive nature of our belief system

Now do the following:

A. At this point in time, on a scale of 1 to 10 (with 10 being the most painful), how painful do you anticipate that childbirth will be for you? (Circle one.)

   1   2   3   4   5   6   7   8   9   10

B. Is this an acceptable pain level for you? Yes No (Circle one.)

C. If your answer to B is no, look back over the five points of comfort and celebration of the life force and write out your beliefs around number 1. Then write out the myths that would be more beneficial to your belief system and make a decision to do whatever it takes to alter your "myth" to bring you closer to your comfort zone.

D. Look at number 4 under comfort and celebration and do what it takes to remember and work on a dream in the next two to four weeks. (See Chapter Eight.)

E. After you have completed steps A through D, take ten minutes to go off to your stoop, or a gentle place in nature and address number 5. You may do this by again writing out your desirable beliefs, this time in an affirmative form. *Example:* I have accepted my ambivalence surrounding being a mother, and I have let go of my fear and judgment surrounding this ambivalence. It is normal to feel this way. The best that I can do is to become aware of my purpose in life, my need for support, play, and exercise, and to nurture myself in all these areas to the best of my ability. I have also opened myself to both physical and emotional help from wherever it flows. Taking care of myself to the best of my ability, I am now able to nurture my baby freely and willingly. I accept my own need for nurturance. I accept that I am a loving and fallible human being.

Chapter Eleven

PUTTING IT ALL TOGETHER

PERSONAL PLANS FOR PREGNANCY AND LABOR

The preparation for your labor and your birth should ideally begin three months prior to conception. If you are like most parents, however, you didn't begin until you found out you were pregnant. The pregnancy health plan is designed to help you use all parts of the Leclaire Method in an organized way throughout your pregnancy so that labor, when it arrives, is just an intensified version of what you have been doing all along.

One of the classes I teach, the Saturday Smart Beginnings class, is a one-day, all-day pregnancy retreat. We meet from 10:30 to 5:30 in a sacred Native Indian healing ground. In this class we use all of the techniques, and the day mimics labor in that the support person is there 100 percent, and both mother and father are in a semitrance or deep hypnotic state all day. We go through early labor and transition and employ all the techniques for these stages. Mothers and fathers then realize that labor is just an extension of the Saturday Smart Beginnings. The day of birth is another day of concentration, with focused attentiveness of the support person to the mother—a lovely, special dress rehearsal in a hypnotic trance.

Like this "dress rehearsal" for the labor and birth of your baby, the months of pregnancy are preparation for the healthy life we all wish for our children. The added bonus for mothers is that this health plan is a good and easy regimen to follow for their own good health. Not only will you nourish your uborn, preparing your baby to have healthy cells for a long life, but you'll be building your own body's health.

While you are preparing, indulge yourself in a sensual and relaxing experience. Here are a few ways to do this:

- *Feet:* Walk your own path. What does that mean to you?
- *Legs:* Support yourself and get proper support from others.
- *Hands:* Reach out and hold onto what you want and need. Let go of what you don't need or want.
- *Arms:* Comfort and embrace yourself, your baby, and others whom you choose.
- *Shoulders:* Carry what you want and need. Let go of the rest. Ask your own inner guide or your own higher power for the wisdom to know the difference.
- *Eyes:* See what you choose to see. Fill your eyes with beauty. Choose your literature, television, and movies carefully. Spend as much time as you can in nature in the midst of wherever you are. While you're pregnant, make a list of what you want to show your baby.
- *Mouth:* Eat well and slowly in a relaxing environment. Kiss often and speak kind, gentle, and compassionate words. Talk and read to your baby.
- *Ears:* Listen to the people and music and sounds you enjoy. Do not listen to any scary pregnancy or birthing stories. If people volunteer stories that make you in the least uncomfortable, politely stop them and excuse your-

self. Do not watch movies or videos of other women's birth experiences. These can set you up for failure or fear.

- *Your mind's eye:* Create your own images of your perfect birth. Use imagery to contribute to your own comfort and healing. Visualize the pregnancy, labor, birth, and postpartum that you desire.
- *Your anchor:* Circle this point on your chest throughout your pregnancy so that it works for you whenever you need it to.

YOUR PERSONAL PREGNANCY HEALTH PLAN

Developing your health plan is the most effective way to maintain your health throughout your pregnancy and to prepare for your labor, birth, and postpartum. It is a good idea to write your plan in pencil so that you can make any changes you might choose or need. All of your life will now be broken into six categories:

- *Creative thinking,* which includes meditation, imagery, and hypnosis.
- *Exercise,* which includes walking, yoga, stretching, and swimming.
- *Social support,* including your partner, family, friends, church, temple groups, group therapy, individual therapy, childbirth classes, obstetrician, midwife, and doula (an experienced woman companion in attendance to the mother at all stages of labor through birth). Some studies show that when a trained birth attendant comforts the mother throughout labor, cesarean section is reduced by 50 percent, the length of labor is reduced by 25 percent, the use of pitocin by 40 percent, and the request for epidurals by 60 percent.
- *Nourishment,* including proper healthy food and nourishment of the senses through touch, hearing, smell, and sight.

- *Play,* which includes anything that brings a sense of joy and freedom and is not goal oriented. As part of your play, you might choose to make a play list just for fun.
- *Purpose in life,* which evolves throughout our lives. Our purpose in life changes over time.

All of these categories are important, but you should not allow one to take over all others. Many women, for example, feel an urge to change their living environment. I have consistently noticed pregnant mothers needing to either redecorate or remodel their homes during pregnancy. This is related to life purpose, with adjustments to the home to fulfill the needs of the new family and the new life. This rearranging of the home may also have something to do with a desire for control when life seems a bit out of control and/or the instinctual nesting behavior. You and your partner, and perhaps your family, are undergoing changes out of your immediate control. There are new rules, new relationships; life is in flux.

Be careful. Redecorating or creating a nursery can be fun—but remodeling while pregnant (when living in the home that is being remodeled) usually causes much stress and can lead to preterm labor. Take good care as you decide what your purpose in life is during your pregnancy. It could be just to write in your pregnancy diary on a daily basis to bond with your baby, or it could be to eat the freshest, healthiest foods to build the health of your uborn's body and mind.

Case Study: Annelise

Annelise is one such mother who believed that her life purpose was to remodel her home. She had been placed on bed rest because she had had preterm labor. Even on bed rest, though, this pregnant mother was supervising a major remodel of her home. After living under these conditions for five months, she had realized she couldn't tolerate it and moved to her brother's home.

I was called to make a home visit to Annelise during her sixth month of pregnancy. At the time, she, her husband, and her two-year-old were staying at her brother's house for two weeks. After that she moved to a friend's house for another two weeks and then back again to her brother's. She was able to carry her baby to term, but she didn't enjoy her pregnancy or her two-year-old son during the process of remodeling. She was exhausted and had severe prenatal anxiety.

Annelise's behavior is part of what I could almost call a syndrome of modern-day nesting. I have heard similar stories from multitudes of mothers. It would be much healthier for the mother to bring the baby home to a smaller, not-so-modern house than to remodel during a time when serenity is the main purpose.

EXERCISE: PUTTING YOUR PLAN TOGETHER

When you are putting together your pregnancy plan, and especially when you think about your life's purpose, keep in mind the following simple rules:

- Make your goals easier to meet than not to meet.
- Honor your own personality.
- Do not overwhelm yourself or set yourself up for failure.
- Be gentle with yourself.
- Make your goals measurable.
- Have fun and enjoy your plan. Play with it and be creative.

A SAMPLE PREGNANCY HEALTH PLAN

One woman made the following plan to help her through her pregnancy. If you adapt such a plan, make adjustments as seem appropriate to meet your personal needs.

SAMPLE PREGNANCY HEALTH PLAN

	FIRST TRIMESTER	SECOND TRIMESTER	THIRD TRIMESTER	THREE MONTHS POSTPARTUM
Creative Thinking	Listen to pregnancy tape once a week.	Learn meditation; meditate once a week for twenty minutes; listen to pregnancy tape two times each week; keep a dream journal two nights each week.	Meditate for twenty minutes two times each week; listen to pregnancy tape four times a week; during thirty-ninth week, listen to labor tape every day.	Meditate every day for first ten days; play music tape daily for at least one feeding with baby.
Social Support	Spend time with partner daily, five minutes of holding each other; dinner together with candles at least once each week; lunch with girlfriend once each week; choose a midwife.	Continue same as first trimester, plus find another mother who is doing this method and invite her to listen to tape together once a week; visit with someone in extended family once a week.	Continue same as second trimester, plus attend Saturday Smart Beginnings class or another class. Find a friend or professional to be a labor companion.	Spend time daily with partner; ten minutes holding each other; call or see members of family circle for at least ten minutes three times for at least a total of one-half hour each day.
Nutrition	Take prenatal vitamins daily; begin to gather information about nutrition and reread nutrition chapter in this book.	Eat sitting down; chew food slowly and well; unplug the phone and turn off television while eating.	Continue as second trimester, and eat from chosen nutrition plan from each food group.	Eat nourishing foods; eat three meals a day; arrange to have meals prepared by family, friends, or professionals.

Exercise	Find a yoga class or swimming pool; take a ten-minute walk three times each week.	Swim or practice yoga or both two times each week; take a ten-minute walk five times each week.	Swim or do yoga three times each week for twenty minutes; walk three times each week for twenty minutes.	Walk outside for ten minutes every day; do two sun salutations (or another yoga pose) each day.
Play	Go to a jazz or classical music concert once a month; plan a weekend trip.	Take a weekend trip; read one novel a month; listen to music twice a week.	Plan a local day trip to a park or another natural setting; continue reading novels and listening to music; enjoy breakfast in bed once a month.	Rock in rocking chair and listen to music; buy flowers and rest and look at their colors and beauty; go out to lunch with a friend once a week when baby reaches eight weeks old.
Purpose in Life	Reread one chapter in this book each week; write a pregnancy diary five minutes every day; work at my profession six hours each day four days a week.	Go back and do exercises in this book once each week; continue to write in pregnancy diary five minutes each day; work at profession three hours a day, five days each week.	Continue as before, following the rest of health plan; decorate nursery; go to breast-feeding class; work at profession three hours a day five days a week.	Sleep as much as possible; feed and massage and care for baby; feed and massage and care for self; remain calm.

Remember, this is just a sample health plan. Please take your health plan seriously, but make it fun to do. The father or partner can make his or her own plan; it doesn't have to match yours. After you each complete your plans, share them and discuss them with each other. Make an extra copy and put your plans on the refrigerator so you can easily check on yourself. Support each other in following through with your desires. Don't nag or push; just gently help each other to succeed in your desires. Not only will completing and using this plan on a daily basis make your pregnancy go more smoothly, *it can help prevent postpartum depression.* See Appendix, page 231, for an exercise on creating a personal plan for easy labor.

EXERCISE: CREATING A PERSONAL PLAN FOR EASY LABOR

Now that you have created a health plan for pregnancy, it is a good idea to begin to explore your desires about your upcoming labor. Here are a few suggestions and ideas for how you can experience this.

If you haven't already done all the exercises in this book, including writing out your own health plan, do so now. Make a list of questions for your midwife or obstetrician regarding anything at all. The following are a few frequently asked questions that may be helpful to you as you prepare your own list:

- What is your rate of cesarean sections?

- Do you automatically give an episiotomy?

- I intend to use all the techniques of the Leclaire Method for concentration and pain relief. How do you feel about that?

- If I change my mind, what kind of anesthesia do you offer? What are the side effects?

- I prefer to move around during labor. I expect to do things like sit on a toilet through most of the second stage and to squat when I birth. How do you feel about that?

- If there is no medical emergency, I would like my baby put on my belly and on my breast immediately so she can nurse and my uterus can contract naturally. How do you feel about that?

- For second stage, some of the other positions I may like are standing and leaning on the bed rail and swaying back and forth, rocking in a rocking chair, or being in a semisitting position with my legs pulled back. I may prefer half-kneeling, half-squatting, or having one leg squatting and one leg supported on a bolster or pillows, alternating the squatting leg periodically. What do you think of these positions? Do you have any good positions that you might suggest so I can try them out ahead of time?

Decide who you would like to have with you in the birthing room. A professional female companion, or doula, can offer great benefits to mothers and their partners. If you have a midwife, you can usually forego the doula. The fewer people in the room with you, the easier it will be for you to relax and concentrate.

Decide whom you want in the hospital waiting room. One mother I know, Jill, said that even the thought of her mother-in-law in the vicinity of the hospital would inhibit her labor. She and her husband, Tom, decided not to tell Tom's mother that they were in the hospital until the baby was born.

Choose what you would like to wear during labor. One mother, Rosalinda, came from a Catholic-Latin background. She felt that being too exposed, too unclothed, would inhibit her labor. She was a petite woman and decided to wear just an extra large cotton T-shirt and cotton leggings with no panties attached to them. She broke in the T-shirt ahead of time. You may think this is a trivial concern, when you're imagining the excitement in the birthing room, but you need to think about anything that may be important to you and address those concerns ahead of time. You're preparing for the birth, and that should include making yourself as comfortable as possible, including choosing whether you'll wear a T-shirt or some other garment that will allow you to birth your baby and bring you a sense of security and comfort.

Choose what you would like to bring to the birthing room. Mothers I know have brought cotton balls soaked with aromatherapy scents, such as rosewater or lavender; photographs or drawings of nature or a favorite natural setting; honey and fresh lemon to add to warm water to sip throughout labor; a carton of fresh white or light miso soup to have in the refrigerator (this can be added one teaspoon to one cup of boiling water and dissolved to sip for energy and to balance your metabolism during the first stage of labor). Some women bring tape decks and play their *Leclaire Smart Beginnings Music* tape or other music; others bring their *Hypnosis for Labor* tape, which can help them relax and center themselves. The tapes are best to listen to when you first arrive at the birthing room. After that, if you feel like it, play them intermittently. You may prefer to use your anchor and your support person's voice to soothe and center you, however. You may want to bring a candle, food for the support person to snack on, and anything else that may increase the comfort of either of you, such as face cream, toothbrush and toothpaste, sesame or olive oil for massage, and a nightgown for after the baby arrives. Ghee (clarified butter) is an excellent salve to prevent your nipples from cracking during and after nursing. It is okay for the baby to ingest this if some is left on the nipples when he nurses.

During labor:

- Play your tape at early first stage.

- Take warm baths before your water breaks.

- Take warm showers.

- Keep active during early labor. If it is night, just sleep and relax during contractions.

Drawing Your Plans

Now that you have read most of this book and written your plans and goals, go back and do the drawings as discussed in Chapter Two with your support person. As you come closer to the birth of your baby, you will gain confidence by facing your fears. As with Karin and Kim (see page 26), you may be able to adjust your plans and your baby to have the birth you desire. Now, given your new understanding of the process, your drawings will reflect the confidence and peace you are creating.

Chapter Twelve

ZEN AND THE ART OF LABOR

YOUR BABY'S MAGIC CARPET RIDE

When you begin the first stage of your labor, find a comfortable place to rest and begin your usual meditation practice. Don't be overly concerned if your mind seems unfocused and wanders; you won't be able to control all of these wanderings, nor should you try. Just remain present in the moment and observe; you will be in complete awareness of every moment of your labor. You will be totally present in the now, aware of the meandering thoughts and of the physiology of your birthing process.

Following is an example of what your thoughts might be like during labor:

Ah, yes, I am breathing in and out and in again and out again. Hmmmm, yeah. I am having a contraction. I feel my belly rising. I feel it from the inside. I think I'll place my hands on my abdomen. I feel it from the outside, and I am breathing in and out and in and out like I have since I was born. No change, yet many changes.

My mind is wandering. I wonder where it's going—oh, it is listening to the horses' rhythmic walking gait down the road, and I am hearing someone cough outside. I feel a bit dizzy, a bit light-headed. I am still. I am warm. I am sleepy. I breathe in. I have as long as I have before I give birth. Can I do this? Can I stay in the moment? My breath is comforting. It continues without me. Perhaps if I become aware of it.

Perhaps if I become like my breath, consistent in and out and in and out no matter what. In and out no matter what, in and out. My eyelids are heavy. I feel a gentle breeze. My breath is the breeze. I'm falling into a trance. I'm falling asleep. Oh, I'm having another contraction. My uterus is like my breath, now rhythmical. I wonder how many breaths before the next contraction and how many during this one. I'm rising and rising, like a loaf of bread in fast frame, only I feel slow. Oh, I've risen, now I'm subsiding, releasing. Down the birth canal you go, one breath at a time, one contraction at a time. This is interesting. I'm here, I'm groggy, I'm in a trance, I'm falling asleep.

Oh, am I dreaming? I must have slept. I feel my breath, I feel my contraction, I feel my breath in and out, in and out, in and out, in and out, in and out, in and out. I think that was thirty breaths to this contraction. I wonder when I should call John and how long it will take him to get here. I wonder when we should go to the birthing room. Oh, I guess I'll call him now. He'll be here in half an hour. I feel so stable observing my breath and my contractions. My mind is wandering. Should I be aware of its wandering? Oh, now that I am aware I can bring my focus back to my breath. I'm breathing in; I'm breathing out.

I guess that's all labor is. It's like life; things happen, life enters, and I keep breathing as I have since I was born, in and out, only now I'm not waiting for anything. I need to not await the next contraction. I need to just be here and now. Oh, I hear the crickets. I'm walking down the path by the creek, I'm five, and I'm with my grandfather, and we're going fishing, and the crickets are singing. Where did I go? Oh! I was in the room of remembrance. I am smiling. I'm back to my breath, no distraction for a while, just breathing in and breathing out. Another contraction. I observe myself in my body, my uterus in my body, my baby in my uterus, my belly rising, and I just continue to breathe, and I feel peaceful, serene. I see my peace; I see my serenity. I'm not there yet; my eye is still here observing, and I am observing it observing me.

Oh, shut up. You are human, what do you expect? Oh, compassion, that's right. I am doing the best that I can do. All I have to do is keep doing what I'm doing. I have done this all my life. The only difference is that now I am paying attention to my breath, to my body, to my thinking.

Soon, perhaps, I won't be aware of my practice of turning my attention to my breath. Soon perhaps I will be my breath like I was for a second before when I thought I was the breeze and the breeze was my breath. Is there truly a medical condition of pain in childbirth, or is it my ego's involvement in my suffering? I've dealt with this during my pregnancy; now I have a chance to not participate in my own suffering. I want to accept this entire labor as the process of giving birth to my baby. Nothing more, nothing less. If I can remain in the now throughout the process of my labor, I will experience a process of transformation. But my goal can't be the desire for transformation, for that takes me out of the now. I am; my body is. I am here; he is here; we are here. I bet my baby isn't thinking what's next. I bet he is just enjoying now. He probably isn't labeling his flow through the birth canal as enjoyment. I bet he is just where he is in the birth. He just is during the contractions and he just is during the relaxation and he just is during the next contraction and the next relaxation. He doesn't feel the feeling, and he doesn't label the contact of being pushed through the birth canal.

He is aware of the contact. But is he conscious of the awareness, and does he recognize that he is aware and conscious and that what he is experiencing is a passage through the birth canal? I don't imagine that he has recognition of the experience. But it takes recognition to feel things. Then we label that recognition as pleasant, unpleasant, or neutral. I think my baby doesn't have recognition yet. However, he can feel—not through his recognition, but through mine. My biochemistry of any negative or positive feelings is experienced by his biochemistry. Therefore, I have a responsibility not to judge this process, not to recognize the experience of this process. I have a responsibility to maintain a now trance, and when I do so, my baby can be in his normal nirvana state. I would like to have a pain-free, easy, vaginal birth. I am doing what I can now to attain that, and I am not attached to the outcome. Sounds good. Let's see what happens when I get to transition.

I'm now in the birthing room. That transition from home to hospital was easy. See, I'm so used to labeling everything. I see my room. I see my husband. He has gotten so good at just being present, being in the now with me. He sits here in silence with me. I like his hand on my hand now. Before, I didn't like how he rubbed my arm, and I told him and he wasn't offended. He just stopped. He's not attached to how he has to be here. He was in the past willing to be here, and now he's just here, not willing, not unwilling, just here. I feel safe and comfortable. We have no stress. We are just here together.

This contraction is huge, like a tidal wave. Now, squeeze my damn ankle. "Focus on your ankle." I hear him saying this to me. My ankle, my ankle. His hand, my ankle. I am relaxing my jaw, my hands. His hand and my abdomen, my contraction and his hand are one. I feel his hand. I feel his hand, I feel, I breathe his hand. It's over. I'm falling asleep.

Another contraction; should I feel my belly? I hear John: "Relax your jaw. Where is your breath?" Where is my breath? Is he nuts? See your breath as sound. Be inside the sound. In sound. Aum, eum, ium, oum, uum.

Breathe in sound. Breathe out sound, leg squeeze, contraction rising, rising.

Circle on my chest, finger on my upper lip, press, squeeze my ankle. Easy does it transition. I'm falling asleep.

Another one. This works; my mouth is open. I make sounds and put my hand over my mouth and my upper lip like I've seen the American Indians do, chanting rhythmically: Wah wah wah wah wah wah wha wha wha wha wha wha wah wahwah, whaaaaa.

If you have participated in the methods of this program, you can expect to and believe and be able to do the following:

1. Participate fully in your pregnancy, labor, and birth.
2. Relax when making your anchor circle on your chest.
3. Relax completely during early contractions.
4. Stay focused and participate as the rhythmic risings, or contractions, become more intense.
5. Understand the purpose of contractions and the importance of focus and work.

6. Succeed at relaxing your jaw and your hands throughout your labor.
7. Concentrate on your ankle as your support person squeezes it during transition.
8. Breathe naturally. Your body automatically inhales. You control your exhalation. You will be able to send your exhalation all the way through your body, down through your spine and out through your cervix and vagina.
9. Position yourself and empty your bladder frequently throughout labor.
10. Stay in touch with your intuition throughout your pregnancy, labor, and birth. If you have an intuition, you will be able to share it with your doctor or midwife.
11. Find a comfortable birthing position for you and your baby.
12. Have a calm, centered, easy vaginal birth.
13. Have your baby on your belly and at your breast immediately after birth.
14. Allow your baby to suckle, which will help with easy delivery of the placenta, with little or no bleeding.
15. Continue caring for yourself and nourishing yourself through all of your senses and by maintaining good social support (even if it is professional) during your postpartum.
16. If you have postpartum blues or depression, immediately seek help by talking with your family, friends, and/or a professional; giving yourself a daily massage; or asking for a massage from family and/or professionals. You might also consult with an Asian medicine practitioner for acupuncture or perhaps herbal therapy. (Acupuncture is highly effective for restoring the physiological balance of your body postpartum, thus preventing or eliminating postpartum problems.) After the baby arrives, continue to eat well and get as much sleep as possible, or at least enough rest.

PLANNING ATTAINABLE GOALS

The easiest way to attain your goals is to define and simplify them. For the best results, plan goals that are easy to meet rather than difficult. Kim's story is a good example of setting attainable goals for success.

Case Study: Kim

Kim was pregnant with her third child. Her first two children had been in posterior position and induced. Even when these babies were nearing their due dates, they had not positioned themselves in the uterus to enter the birth canal in the proper way; they were faced forward. This position makes the birth more difficult for both mother and baby. It means that the baby will be born face up, not face down, as is the normal position. (See Chapter Two for the drawing Kim did.)

Kim and I worked together to set goals for the labor and birth of her third child. These are the goals she set:

1. To do all that she could do naturally to turn Karin (the name she had chosen for her uborn) around.
2. To do all that she could to prevent having labor induced and the use of pitocin. To be able to feel when to push.
3. To be able to comfortably push when necessary.

Kim's previous pregnancies and labor influenced her goals. During the labor for her second child, she hadn't been able to feel and couldn't push because of her epidural. This time she wanted to do all that she could to prevent an epidural. Kim's goals were not unrealistic—nor were they necessarily the same goals that you would set for your own labor and the birth of your child. But they did improve upon her previous experiences and give her a sense of control over the labor and birth that she had not had during her previous pregnancies.

I met with Kim only during the last three weeks of her pregnancy, because she had not heard about the program until then. Even though she was due in a very short time, she wanted to try her best to be more aware of the birth of Karin, and she was motivated to make this happen. We met once a week up until Kim's due date. We discussed her goals; these were not clear to her when we first met. As she clarified them, she seemed to relax and become less agitated.

The first week we met, after we discussed the techniques and principles of meditation, Kim and I meditated together. She was able to say her mantra and focus on it for twenty minutes. She felt a great sense of accomplishment that enabled her to believe that she might be able use all the other tools and principles successfully. Between our visits, she listened to her hypnosis and pregnancy tapes daily and even learned to meditate for the first time, although she had tried unsuccessfully in the past.

The second time we met, she had just come from her doctor. He had told her that Karin was, in fact, posterior. Kim drew a picture of Karin in utero and another of her being born in a posterior position. Then she drew a picture of Karin in the proper position in utero and during birth.

We discussed these positions, and Kim said, "Maybe she just wants to be born face up so she can see us right away. Maybe her personality is like my two-year-old's, and she is assertive and needs what she needs immediately."

We talked about the position of the baby and also about ways Kim might influence the baby's position. I told her that many mothers had positioned themselves down on all fours and that that position helps a baby turn from posterior position naturally. Kim placed her hands on her belly and talked with Karin: "Karin, it is lovely that you want to look into my face immediately. However, I want this to be the best birth possible for both of us, and the position that you are in now is not necessarily the best one. If you don't arrive exactly on your due date, you will be induced. And that is not the best procedure for either one of us. So please turn around. You don't have to do it right now, but I'm going to get down on all fours three times a day. While I'm on all fours, I'll continue to explain to you why it is important for you to turn."

Kim then got down on all fours in my office, and I put my hand on her belly and spoke to Karin. Then Kim and I continued to discuss her needs. She decided that she would like to have a registered nurse trained in the Leclaire Method present at her birth. This would be her own private nurse and support person, someone who was there to help her obtain her goals for labor and who understood techniques that could help her attain those goals. I suggested a nurse I knew and had trained, Lorraine. Kim thought that Lorraine could also be a support to her husband, which would help him, in turn, be more supportive to Kim. As we parted, Kim agreed to listen to her tapes again and to discuss the private nurse with her husband. Kim's husband, Joe, was already a naturally supportive person and wanted Kim to have a better experience during this labor and birth, so he agreed to have Lorraine present.

On the third visit, Kim arrived with her husband so that he, too, could learn the techniques. If he knew the techniques, he could better support her during labor, and Lorraine could guide them both in techniques he didn't know or remember. We now had only one hour for her husband to learn how to be the perfect support person during labor. Luckily, Joe had listened to the tapes and was open and eager to help Kim have the birth she wanted. As I've discovered, most humans are like this. We typically leave things to the last minute, even (and sometimes especially) important decisions. A good part of learning any new skill is believing that we can accomplish what we set out to learn, however. Trust, desire, expectation, and motivation are all crucial to the process of learning. (Motivation is certainly increased when cramming for anything, especially labor. "Hurry up and learn to relax" sounds absurd, and yet it can—and usually does—work. So don't be overly concerned about when you start the process. Just start it.)

Joe began trying to help Kim relax by manifesting his presence. He did this by slowly moving his hands from her head to her feet, about one inch above her body. He focused all his energy completely on hers, not touching her but moving his hands slowly, one inch from her body, using the focus of his mind to send his energy toward her. He and she both thought about their energy meeting. Kim closed her eyes softly, and a peaceful silence ensued. This is a lovely beginning as a mother goes into labor, and Joe now had the experience of doing it in an easy environment. Now he would be ready to repeat this at the crucial time as labor began.

Next Joe put his hands gently on Kim's body, starting with her forehead. He moved his fingers back and forth across her forehead and then massaged her entire head, face, and body in long, downward strokes, in a similar manner. This is a method that any support person can use during the early stage of labor.

After Joe finished the gentle and silent massage, he and Kim practiced the transition technique. (See page 56.) We did not have time to do a complete introduction and training in hypnobirthing, but because Kim had been playing her tape, she knew that her anchor (see page 69) worked very well for her. She made the circle on her chest with the middle finger of her left hand. When she was in a deep trance, she dropped her hand. Joe looked at her and said his labor mantra. (See page 146.) I had just explained this to him briefly as Kim made her anchor. His mantra went something like this: "Good. You are very relaxed. Keep your jaw relaxed and your hands relaxed. Breathe all the way through your body and send the breath out through your vagina."

During transition, most mothers don't like to be touched or rubbed; rubbing at that point can be irritating rather than comforting, except for the ankle technique, as practiced for transition in Chapter Eight. Later, as Kim's abdomen would rise during transition with the rhythmic rise of her uterine muscle,[1] Joe would squeeze her ankle harder and harder so that Kim, with her jaw and hands relaxed, could focus her attention on her ankle. This would greatly enhance her ability to focus through transition without any pain medication.

Joe practiced, and then I counted Kim back up from her trance, and he squeezed her ankle again. Like all mothers, she was amazed at the difference in the sensation when in a trance and not in a trance.

Because Joe and Kim had arrived late and were on a tight schedule—and because I had another patient arriving soon—we had little time and had to do things more quickly than usual. I discovered that we could accomplish a lot, even if time was short. We had about seven minutes left, and Joe read aloud the list describing how to be a good support person. (See pages 204–205 and 208–209.) We briefly discussed one or two of these suggestions. With a little more than one minute to go in our session, Kim asked me to explain the Leclaire philosophy to Joe. She thought this an impossible task and grinned at me as she asked me to do it. My reply was that it is a very simple concept and that it actually only takes about one minute to explain. As I told Joe, our bodies know exactly how to birth our babies, just as Earth knows exactly how to give blossoms to the flowers. All we have to

---

1. Although these rhythmic risings are commonly called contractions, this term has negative connotations for most women. Picture them as waves of rising and falling instead.

do is to keep our mind out of our bodies' way long enough for the body to do the work it knows so well how to do. They listened, smiled, agreed, and said that somewhere along the way we had forgotten all of that.

As they were leaving, Kim returned to an earlier discussion we had had about acupuncture. We had talked about how acupuncture can initiate labor. Kim decided to contact a Chinese medical doctor she knew to meet her at the hospital on Monday, her due date. That way she could have labor induced by acupuncture if necessary.

Kim's ultimate goal, of course, was for her and her new baby Karin to be healthy and safe. She had done all that she could in the short period of time that we had to accomplish her goals.

On the Monday morning of her due date, Kim stopped in at her acupuncturist's office first and then went to the hospital to meet her doctor. Her doctor was pleased to discover that the baby was no longer posterior. Kim later told me that she was pretty sure she knew the time when her baby had turned. She had been on all fours, meditating in that position, when she felt the baby shift position. She can't be sure, but she thinks that is when it happened.

The doctor wanted to do a light induction, even though the baby had turned into the correct birthing position. At Kim's insistence, she was given only a very light dose of the drug to induce labor. She had arrived at the hospital around 10:30 A.M., and by 4:30 that afternoon she held her newborn daughter in her arms. She told her doctor, after the birth, "Michelle Leclaire O'Neill is a witch! She helped me have exactly the birth I wanted. I wanted to feel the baby moving through me, and I felt her. I wanted to push her out and feel myself pushing her out, and I did."

Although Kim did request a light epidural, she still had enough sensation to feel the contractions and feel herself pushing the baby through the birth canal. She described the contractions and the labor as "very comfortable," and when I looked at the pictures she had drawn, I saw that she had met her goals.

For a mother of two previous children, this was a breakthrough—that she could plan and help to control the labor process. Even with only three weeks to prepare and a backlog of prenatal anxiety from her past experience, Kim was able to accomplish her goal of a birth she was fully present for and an experience she will be able to fully remember.

TIPS FOR LABOR

We'll now go through the rest of labor so you will know how to use your techniques, not just for the dress rehearsal but for opening night. During labor and birth, you should not be left alone. You should have all the support possible and all the support you desire. Cooperation among obstetrician, midwife, father, and other support people creates a perfect scenario for an easy birth.

The First Stage of Labor: Contractions

The purpose of labor is to pull the cervix wide so that the baby can make her way from the womb into the world and into her mother's arms. As the uterus tightens and relaxes (in what we commonly call a *contraction*), the cervix becomes thin, or effaces, and then opens, or dilates. This is the longest part of labor, as the uterine muscle pulls the cervix open. Once the cervix is dilated to about seven centimeters, the second stage of labor, transition, begins.

How long it takes for the cervix to open to seven centimeters varies. As long as you have a professional such as a physician or a midwife attending you, time is not important. It takes as long as it takes. The Leclaire Method both shortens the first stage of labor and helps the time seem to pass rapidly, however. If you use these techniques, you may not even raise the question of time, because that will not be your focus. Many mothers report that time seems to be suspended during this phase, much as it is during a runner's high or during sleep or other meditative states.

Because the purpose of the first stage of labor is to open the cervix for the baby to arrive, your job during this period is to relax your mind, your body, and your vaginal area. Only through this relaxation will the muscles allow the expansion to happen.

You may be asking yourself how you will know you are in labor. The second question will be: What do I do?

If you have reached full term for your pregnancy and contractions begin, the best way to differentiate between real and false labor is to walk about, shower, take a warm bath, or simply change position frequently by squatting or otherwise moving. If the contractions get stronger and closer together, you are probably in labor.

As the contractions begin, it is a good idea to record each contraction, or rhythmic rising of the uterus, writing down the time each begins and the length of each one. This allows your midwife or physician to assess how your labor is progressing. If your amniotic sac (bag of waters) breaks, either before or during labor, record the time and also the amount and color of the fluid. Notify your health care professional immediately. Do not take a bath after the membrane has ruptured, although it is all right to take a shower.

Early Stage One Labor

In early labor, your contractions, or rhythmic risings, may last twenty to sixty seconds and occur at intervals of five to twenty minutes. The following are things you should do during this period:

1. Continue to record the contractions, writing down the length and the time elapsed between contractions.
2. Lie down.
3. Listen to your labor tape.
4. Empty your bladder at least once each hour.
5. Put on soothing music and move or dance to it slowly.
6. Ask your support person to give you a massage.
7. Take a warm (not hot) bath or shower.
8. Meditate for twenty minutes every two hours.
9. Walk, squat, and move about.
10. Rock in a rocking chair or glider.
11. Give yourself a massage.
12. Stay present in the now.
13. Sip warm water or miso soup. (Avoid cold drinks, ice chips, or other snack foods; these are not relaxing.)
14. Suck on a lollipop.

Late Stage One Transition

The transition period begins when your cervix is dilated to between seven and ten centimeters. During this period, there are things to do during contractions and things to do between contractions. During contractions, remain in the now. Stay focused. Do not think; just be with the moment. Visualize your cervix opening like a flower, the petals slowly and gently opening wider and wider. Visualize your baby sliding down and out through your body. Have your support person use the ankle squeeze technique during each contraction as a safe ritual that you can count on and that you know well from practice (see page 146). During each contraction:

1. Relax your jaw; relax your hands.
2. Breathe. Your breath will be natural and automatic if you remain relaxed in a trance.

3. Use sounding during your contraction: Aum, eum, ium, oum, uum. Or call it a "rhythmic rising" and repeat, "I am having a rhythmic rising."

Between contractions, or rhythmic risings:

1. Rest, sleep, and meditate.
2. Move about to find the most comfortable position.
3. Take a sip of warm (room temperature) water or miso soup after each contraction.
4. Empty your bladder every hour.

Late Stage One Labor

This period generally lasts ten to sixty minutes and includes five to twenty contractions. During this period, the support person should follow these guidelines:

1. During contractions: Remain in the room. Be totally present and focused. Remain quiet and serene and serious. Any frivolity now may act as an irritant to the mother.
2. Use the ritual that you established ahead of time during each contraction. Use sounding, and ask the mother to join you: Aum, eum, ium, oum, uum. Repeat your mantra of relaxation: "Good. Now relax your jaw. Relax your forehead. Relax your hands. Good. Relax your jaw."
3. Squeeze the mother's left ankle with your entire hand. (See page 146.) Place your hand about four fingers above the ankle on the inner side of the leg and apply pressure. This is an acupressure point that can reduce pain and enhance opening of the cervix. It also becomes a point of focus for the mother during each contraction, distracting her; the body cannot feel two discomforts at the same time. You should not practice this ankle squeeze technique before the due date, because this pressure point can also cause contractions.

4. Remind the mother to use her anchor—her circle on her chest—to deepen her hypnotic state.

5. Encourage and reassure her that she is now making more rapid progress.

6. Do not discuss time. Stay at one with the moment.

7. Offer a sip of warm (room temperature) water or miso soup after each contraction.

8. Let the mother rest, meditate, or sleep between contractions, and you do the same.

9. Don't leave her during this stage. If you have to empty your bladder, have someone stand in for you with the mother.

10. Encourage her to empty her bladder every hour.

11. Do not rush her. This can act as an irritant.

12. For back labor or pain, do deep tissue kneading of her buttocks or deep counterpressure. Have the mother kneel and rest, leaning forward on an ottoman. Support the person. Place open palms on outer aspect of the mother's buttocks. Squeeze buttocks together while simultaneously lifting them up toward the spine. This offers an amazing relief from back pressure.

13. Try to prevent any interruptions from hospital staff or others during this period.

14. Keep the room quiet and dim the lights. Peace is imperative.

15. Have the mother sniff a cotton ball with several drops of rosewater on it as the contractions begin.

16. Do not rub or pat or unconsciously touch her in any way during this phase.

In between contractions, when you are not squeezing her ankle, you may either remove your hand or place it gently and firmly but very still somewhere that is comfortable to the mother. Do not talk or make any moves during this still period.

The Second Stage of Labor: Pushing

A twenty-minute rest usually comes for the mother between the transition stage and the pushing stage of labor. You should enjoy this rest and perhaps even sleep during it. Then the second stage of labor will begin. During this phase, you will be pushing your baby out.

This is the most exciting and pleasurable part of labor. Your uterus automatically pushes your baby down every time it contracts, and you consciously push in sync with your uterus, pushing with your abdominal muscles. Together, you are a team. Pushing is the labor part of labor. Your urge to push will become stronger with each contraction.

During this period, it is still important to relax and focus on the moment. Concentrate on the following actions:

1. Relax your vagina, your perineum, and your rectum. Exhale all the way through your body and out through your rectum and/or your vagina.

2. Find a comfortable position that allows gravity to participate in the urging of your child into the world. Many mothers find the toilet a comfortable place to push. This can work up until the baby crowns (appears at the opening of the vagina); then come off the toilet into a supported squatting position. This supported squatting position is the easiest and most natural position for birthing. Another possible position is on all fours, resting your head on your hands, in your partner's lap, or on a stack of pillows. You can also be in a semisitting position, with your legs pulled up or relaxed, or lying on your side with your legs pulled up.

3. Visualize each contraction during this stage as a beautiful full wave advancing, then cresting, with your baby in his vernix caseosa, his protective coating, wetsuit surfing down through the birth canal with each subsiding flow.

Closer and closer he gets with each magnificent rise and fall of your abdominal wave. With each rhythmic rising of the amniotic surf, he comes closer. Allow this to happen. Release and let go. Breathe and push and sound: "Ha-um. . . ha-um . . . ha-um." "Ha-um" seems to be a comfortable sound to repeat during pushing.

4. Focus your third eye with your eyes closed during pushing. The third eye is the space between your eyebrows that many traditions believe is a bridge into your unconscious mind. This can be very effective.

5. Play your music tape softly during this phase (or any phase) if you find it soothing. Some mothers listen to *Leclaire Smart Beginners Music* tape and play the tape over and over and over again, lowering the volume as the contractions become more intense.

6. Use your anchor. Remain in a trance.

As soon as you can after birth—immediately, if possible—have your baby placed on your abdomen. He will automatically scoot up to your breast and want to suckle.

The baby sucking on your breast helps with the third stage of labor, the delivery of the placenta. The baby at your breast helps to contract your uterus and prevents excessive bleeding. At this time, your midwife or obstetrician will probably massage your uterus, complementing the work of your baby at your breast through further aiding in the firm contraction of your uterus.

Play soothing music and enjoy the scent of rosewater on a cotton ball as you and your partner and your baby greet each other as a family.

The Support Person's Role During the Second Stage

Although not much has changed for the support person during this phase, you should be responsive to the subtle changes in the mother. The following guidelines should help you prepare to be supportive during this phase. You may even want to make yourself a shorthand list to carry on a card to the hospital. The list can help remind you what to do.

1. Continue to encourage the mother.
2. Observe her during contractions; continue to tell her to relax her jaw and her hands.
3. Tell her to relax her vagina and rectum and perineum.
4. Use sounding during contractions: "Aum . . . Eum . . . Ium . . . Oum . . . Uum."
5. Encourage the mother to use her anchor and the circle on her chest and to focus on her third eye. Encourage her to remain in a trance.
6. Encourage and whisper her through simple visualization. Watch her abdomen as you say this in sync with the rise and fall of her abdomen. Say it softly and slowly: "A grand full wave is rising, rising in your belly. It is cresting, cresting, and now our baby is riding the wave down through the birth canal, down and out, down and out. Wonderful. Relax your perineum. Relax your jaw and push her closer to birth. Wonderful."
7. Encourage her to close her eyes as the pushing becomes more intense, and to focus on her third eye.
8. Try another visualization, whispering slowly in sync with the rising and falling of her abdomen: "Your belly is rising and falling with a healing white light, a beautiful healing white light. Absorb the healing light and let it guide baby down and out, down and out, down and out. Become at one with the white light and let it surround baby, and let the light flow down through your skull down your spine, and let it surround your uterus and baby, and let it flow with baby down and out of the birth canal. Let your baby be born on a path of this white light. Relax your jaw. Allow your exhalation to flow

down through the birth canal at one with the healing
white light."

9. Stay close by. Help the mother find a comfortable position. Sitting on the toilet can be comfortable until the
baby's head crowns. After crowning, help the mother
move to a squatting position, and hold and support her
in a squatting position or in any position that she chooses
in which gravity is in her favor.

10. Keep the room quiet and serene.

11. Play the music tape softly.

12. Let the mother rest and meditate between contractions.

13. Whenever necessary, count back from ten to one to
deepen her hypnotic state between contractions. Also tell
her, "Your pushing is very effective. Baby is almost here.
Your good, hard work is paying off."

14. Remind the mother to open her eyes as the baby is being
born.

15. Help to put the baby immediately on the mother's
abdomen and to her breast.

16. Tell her you love her, and stay close to them both.

Read over these suggestions and become familiar with them
in the weeks before your baby's birth. All of these suggestions
can help your baby into the world without trauma. It is your task
to make this transition for baby from the womb into your arms as
peaceful as possible, and this requires a peaceful transition for
you as well. You, your spouse, and your baby can experience this
joyful beginning together, mindfully.

Chapter Thirteen

THE RAINBOW AND THE POT OF GOLD

WELCOMING YOUR BABY INTO THE WORLD WHILE MAINTAINING YOUR OWN BALANCE

The intimacy you establish with your uborn will last for your child's lifetime. While that bond remains strong, however, do not let it separate you from the other intimacies that are crucial to your life. Many times husbands feel rejected once the baby arrives. That intimacy can be built while the baby grows within. Don't neglect your other relationships as you focus on your baby. If you have older siblings at home, the way you introduce your newborn to the siblings can affect their relationships for the rest of their lives. Have the father (not the mother) carry the new baby when he is first brought into the house. Try to pay attention to older siblings. Wait for them to ask to see the baby, holding and kissing them and taking their cue.

Case Study: Sam and Rebecca

One father who had attended the class with his wife for the birth of their second and later their third babies showed up for an appointment when baby number three was eight months old. It was a brave thing for him to do. I am certain that many men experience what Sam felt, but not many have the courage to discuss it.

"For the past six years, there has always been a baby at Rebecca's breast. I can never get there. I realize this sounds infantile, but it's the way I feel," he said. To express his needs and to acknowledge them were crucial steps to health and happiness and well-being. After realizing these were normal feelings and not judging them, Sam decided to ask his wife to come in with him for a session. They both arrived with the baby. He was in an infant seat on the floor in front of Rebecca, facing her.

As Sam was explaining his feelings, Rebecca kept smiling and cooing at the baby, finally picking him up to nurse him when he didn't even appear hungry. As a matter of fact, the baby seemed most content.

"See. That is what I mean," said Sam in distress. "Even in here you won't listen to me. I'm trying to explain my needs to you, and you seemingly dismiss them and won't even look at me as I speak. You only have eyes for him!"

Sam was enraged and near tears. Rebecca tried to deny her behavior. As an objective third party, however, I gently explained to her what I saw. She finally relented and said she knew that this was her last child, and she wanted to nurse him as long as possible. It was an intimacy without the demands of an adult relationship. It was relaxing, empowering, and nurturing. Rebecca was truly enjoying the experience more than with her two other children. She felt more relaxed and confident. Nor did she want what felt like another demand on her time and energy by her husband.

They each described their feelings openly. They agreed to plan one date night alone together each week. In addition, they committed to finding time alone each day, even if for only five minutes, to hold each other and demonstrate their appreciation and love for each other. Rebecca agreed to look at Sam when they were speaking and, if she was busy and it was not a good time to talk, to tell him gently and in a loving way. Then they would arrange time later to talk, when she could be more available and attentive to him and his needs. Rebecca also agreed to nurse her new baby until he was two years old instead of until he was three or four, as she had originally planned. Sam and Rebecca now had a family bed—one king-size bed with two single beds on either side. They agreed to discontinue the family bed six months after Rebecca stopped nursing Robert. By that time, the children would sleep in the children's nursery instead of in their parents' room.

They enlisted Sam's parents to watch all three children one night and one day every six weeks. For those times, Rebecca would pump her breast milk, and they would go away overnight together. The children would stay with Sam's parents.

As we talked, it became clear that underlying Rebecca's desire to nurse Robert past two years of age were her own infantile needs. (This is particularly the case in Western culture. In many other countries, it is imperative that a mother continue to nurse her baby until the age of four. In fact, the average age worldwide for discontinuing breastfeeding is four years old.) These needs were not being met. She was also experiencing separation anxiety. Once we discussed her needs and desires for nurturing and mothering, she became able to acknowledge them. By recognizing these needs, she was then able to compromise in her relationship and to understand both Sam and herself without judgment or criticism. Change and compromise work best when we understand the underlying reasons for our feelings and actions. The ability and willingness to make gradual changes and to compromise are at the heart of intimacy.

INTIMACY FOR A LIFETIME

The entire Leclaire Method is based on balancing mind, body, and spirit and listening to your baby, your body, and your loved ones. We can't effectively meet the needs of a newborn without having our own needs met. By listening to our own needs and the needs of others, we can establish a balance between these needs, and we can all feel that we are being heard and that our needs are valid and important. The techniques you've learned in this book will thus help you fulfill the basic requirements of establishing and maintaining intimacy.

By *intimacy*, I mean the ability to understand and respect the essential nature of yourself, your spouse, and your children, combined with the compassion and willingness to create and maintain an environment that fosters the growth and development of each individual and each relationship. Given the demands of a newborn and the emotional and physical strain—including postpartum sleep deprivation—on each member of the family, this can be quite a challenge. With an awareness of the challenge and a bit of preparation, you and your family are capable of the task. The following guidelines should help you prepare yourself and your family for the first three months postpartum.

One thing mothers and fathers should do during the pregnancy is to use the time as a time of bonding, both between partners and with the uborn. Bonding is a time for mothers and fathers to be alone, to be there for each other, not talking about bills or criticizing each other, but rather caressing or massaging each other. It is a time to be together, alone, without the television or telephone.

EXERCISE: DEFINING GOALS AS A COUPLE

The following exercise will bring you closer to who you are, both as mothers and fathers.

Write out your goals around your designs for your life. Write them for now, for six months from now, and for one year from now. Make your goals measurable and easily attainable. Take baby steps rather than giant steps. It is easier to succeed this way.

- Career
- Motherhood
- Fatherhood
- Marriage
- Creativity
- Spirituality
- Nutrition
- Exercise
- Play
- Social support
- Physical contact
- Mental stimulation

After you have finished writing these goals, discuss them with each other.

Start the pattern with a realistic amount of time, even as little as five minutes twice a week, and gradually build to a time that is acceptable to you both. Keep this up during the entire pregnancy and especially during the postpartum, specifically during the first three months after the birth. Be flexible and alter the amount of time as necessary. Be creative, especially after the baby arrives. Fifteen minutes for a walk outside the house may be all the time you feel comfortable leaving the baby with a sitter. Do that for yourself.

Most marital problems, including sexual, are both normal and transitory during pregnancy and the postpartum period.

When the baby is eight to ten months old, all should be back to normal. A mother usually isn't physically recovered until twelve weeks postpartum. She isn't emotionally recovered until eight to ten months after the birth. Take this into consideration when thinking about your sexual patterns and make allowances. The myths and models of our nature that add to our physical, mental, and spiritual well-being are obviously more useful than those that do not. Through knowledge of ourselves and our myths, we may evolve to a oneness of spirit, to that universal truth that lies in each of us.

THE EARLY DAYS OF LIFE AFTER BIRTH

Needs of the Mother

Once your baby has arrived, you will be able to continue your good habits by meditating daily and playing your *Leclaire Smart Beginnings Music* tape. This music is uplifting and will aid in getting your body back in balance. In addition, you should be taken care of by father and other family, friends, or professional support persons for the first ten days postpartum. This should include the following:

- Food should be prepared for you.
- Someone else should clean your house and do the household and baby laundry.
- The father should give you a daily massage, even if for just five minutes. This not only will help you to heal but will enhance the intimacy and love between you.

A new mother's main job, or the purpose of her life for a time, is to bring her body into a state of balance. This is the best way to prevent postpartum depression. During this time, you, the mother, need to concentrate on the following activities:

- Continue eating healthy food. You must remain nourished so that you can breastfeed and care for your new baby.

- Take warm (not hot) baths to release impurities and to relax and rejuvenate.
- Allow yourself to follow a gentle routine that includes rest, nutrition, fresh air, serenity, massage, and meditation.
- If no one is available to give you a massage, massage yourself daily from head to toe.
- Meditate daily.
- Listen to *Leclaire Smart Beginnings Music* (see Resources), as well as other healing music and sounds.
- Sleep.
- Stay close to home, especially for the first ten days. Sit in your garden or on your stoop, porch, roof, or deck. If you do go on an outing, choose someplace in nature.
- Do not overexert yourself.
- Avoid watching or reading the news or any violent television shows or movies.

Father's Work

The father's or partner's main tasks during the first weeks post-partum are to provide as much support and comfort for the mother as possible. Sometimes that support will need to come not only from the father but also from other family members and friends. Mother and father need to accept the generosity and assistance of others during these first few weeks. You can learn to perceive this as support rather than as intrusion. You'll be able to discern the difference by observing carefully and remaining open to the offers others make. When friends and family offer to help, thank them and tell them how much you appreciate their offer. Discuss with the mother each of your needs and then ask for specific ways others can help you fulfill those needs. Be as specific as you can, because others cannot always see what you need. If they can do what you ask, wonderful. Accept their help graciously. If they cannot do what you ask, graciously accept their decline.

One of the father's main goals during this period is to be fully present for the mother and baby whenever needed. Ask the mother frequently if she wants or needs anything and listen attentively when she replies. Wait and listen and then follow through. Constantly reassure her of your love for her. Acknowledge your feelings without being asked. When you say you are going to be present, be 100 percent present and keep your mind focused entirely on the new mother. By turns and as needed, be 100 percent present for yourself, your partner, your baby, and your other children. Treasure each individual and the family as a whole as you welcome the new baby.

Allow an environment of intimacy, love, and support to penetrate and permeate your household. You will be fostering a spirit of working together and loving together as this new life adds a new dimension of promise and growth to your life as a family. This kind of smart beginning can influence a lifetime for all of you.

During this period, the father or other intimate support person must help to coordinate meeting the needs of the mother and baby. To provide this support, the father/support person must first take care of himself/herself by doing the following:

- Eat healthy foods.
- Go to bed early.
- Consider sleeping in another room for up to ten days. Because your new baby will need to sleep near the mother, you may get more rest to fulfill your own work schedule and sleep needs.
- Meditate daily.
- Exercise.
- Accept the support of family and friends. Understand offers of help as support, not intrusion.
- Massage the baby's mother daily for at least five minutes.
- Sit and rest together with the mother and baby. Hold each other and listen to music, or sit in silence, for at least ten minutes each day.

- Give yourself a daily massage. This can take as little as five minutes, but it will aid immeasurably in your own ability to deal with stress and loss of sleep. A quick massage can easily be done first thing when you awake, before you get out of bed.
- Help with diapering, holding, and rocking the baby. Understand the specialness and sacredness of this time you spend with your new child.
- Sleep and nourish yourself.
- Smile and be gentle with yourself and others.
- Make certain that the mother is waited on hand and foot either by you, family, friends, or a professional support person.

Prenatal Anxiety and Postpartum Depression

What our mind doesn't deal with our body does. Our past resounds throughout our cells so that either we need to address the past or it redresses us. Prenatal anxiety and postpartum depression are actually the body's attempt to remedy a situation and to restore wholeness and balance. This is most often an unconscious process. It is a chance for you to bring the reparation to consciousness, however.

By looking more closely at the causes of prenatal anxiety and postpartum depression, we may be able to discover ways to prevent them. Every aspect of the Leclaire Method advocates prevention, and education and prevention may help you prevent both prenatal anxiety and postpartum depression. It appears from my anecdotal research that participating fully in the Leclaire Method can and does contribute to the prevention and treatment of prenatal anxiety and to the prevention and treatment of postpartum depression.

Before describing ways to prevent or treat these, you will need to know what I am talking about. In varying degrees, these are the symptoms exhibited in prenatal anxiety and postpartum depression:

- Labile emotions (fluctuating emotions: one minute you're laughing and the next you're crying, for example)
- Restlessness
- Panic attacks
- Irritability
- Insomnia
- Perseveration (persistent repetition of a thought, an idea, a word, a phrase, or an action)
- Exhaustion
- Confusion
- Hopelessness
- Extreme agitation
- Bizarre behavior and fantasies
- Mania
- Lethargy
- Suicidal ideas
- Ambivalent feelings toward the baby
- Desire to kill or hurt the baby
- Inability to make decisions
- Severe morning sickness
- Loss of appetite
- Anemia
- Isolation behavior
- Refusal to talk about feelings

Many, if not all, of these symptoms are similar to those of other functional disorders. What differentiates these two syndromes from other disorders is that they are triggered by pregnancy and/or birth. They are caused by an imbalance in the mind/body and social structure of the mother. Often they are triggered by poor nutrition, resulting in anemia or sleep deprivation. Ambivalence about your purpose in life and inadequate social support can spiral into these serious conditions, as can lack of human touch, especially the healing touch, and lack of sound. Any of these seemingly "small" omissions in your self-care can culminate in a hormonal imbalance and a general overall physiological and emotional imbalance. Once your system is out of balance, you will experience these symptoms and find yourself sinking more deeply into a sense of despair and a sense of being out of control.

If prenatal anxiety is treated and resolved, there is usually no underlying need, either physical or psychological, for postpartum depression. Once postpartum depression occurs, I believe acupuncture is the most effective treatment. I have observed this with mothers who are in severe, even suicidal postpartum depression. Many have discovered that acupuncture can help heal the physical and psychological aspects of postpartum depression rapidly. Within twenty-four hours of their acupuncture treatment, they feel better. A series of twelve treatments is usually necessary to maintain equilibrium.

Do not take postpartum blues or depression lightly. It occurs more often than the public realizes and is something women have been taught to hide and be ashamed of. We must share these feelings and stories and help each other heal. For more information, see our Web site at http://www.postpartumdepression.org.

Case Study: Cathleen

Up until the time Cathleen became pregnant with her first baby, her marriage was apparently happy. Her husband had a good job that brought him great satisfaction and joy and that also more than adequately compensated him financially. At about the five-month point in her pregnancy, Cathleen quit her job. She tried to maintain contact with her friends at work, and she joined a prenatal yoga group, which gave her more social support. Both her and her husband's families lived thousands of miles away.

Cathleen began to have difficulty sleeping. She also gained more weight than desirable and experienced tremendous fear that either she or her baby would die in childbirth.

After we had been talking together for a few sessions, she told me that her husband was a binge drinker. She didn't care how beautiful her house was or how rich they were; she missed her family and friends, and so did her husband. They had moved to the area and stayed only for his job, and he was willing to move back to their home city, but he wanted her to make the decision.

This responsibility made her feel extremely guilty and froze her ability to make any decisions. She was unable to bond with her baby and was becoming more and more fearful of dying or having a stillborn. Physically she and her baby were progressing well, according to her obstetrician and all the tests. We started to do hypnosis, with the intention of her connecting to her baby in utero so that she could become aware of him as he truly was, healthy or not. I tried to help her go beyond her own anxiety and connect to the baby through her maternal intuition. She drew a picture of him in her belly.

We both loved her drawing of her baby, and together we came up with a darling and playful nickname for him. We discussed him always using that name, even as an adult or on some future job, which made us both smile. This made him more real and alive to her.

After bonding in this way and coming to realize his aliveness, Cathleen began to discuss her feelings of being "abandoned" in a strange city with no support for her husband's drinking except strangers in an Alanon group that she had begun attending. She believed that if she and her husband stayed where they were for the baby's birth, they would be stuck in that city forever.

She then acknowledged another pressure. She wanted to make a decision to birth her baby back in her home city before it was too late to fly. After much deliberation and anxiety, Cathleen told her husband she wanted not only to give birth in their hometown but to move back there. He agreed. It seemed he really wanted to move back, too, but couldn't make the decision himself, which compounded the burden on his wife and the baby. As soon as they put their house up for sale, Cathleen's anxiety diminished greatly.

Later, after her baby was born, we spoke by phone. She also wrote me a wonderful letter telling all about her easy vaginal birth. In the envelope, she enclosed a delightful photo of the little fellow. It resembled the drawing she had made. It was clear that both mother and baby were surrounded by all that was familiar and comfortable and supportive to a new mother, and that this made her happy.

Had Cathleen stayed in California, especially not by conscious choice but by being unable to make any decision, I believe she would have been a likely candidate for a difficult birth and postpartum depression. As this story illustrates, the antecedents of postpartum depression are exhibited in prenatal anxiety. Women can no longer be silent about this. It is my belief that part of prenatal care should be a professional evaluation of the risk of postpartum depression. This evaluation should take place when the mother is in her second or third trimester, and preventive treatment should begin then if treatment hasn't already been incorporated into the preparation for conception.

EFFECTS OF PAST SEXUAL TRAUMA

Often past sexual trauma creates great free-floating anxiety that comes to the forefront during pregnancy. Perhaps the experience has been dealt with in the past, or perhaps it hasn't been. Failure to notice these feelings and connect them to past sexual trauma does not allow for a comfortable labor, pregnancy, and birth.

Denial is an integral part of the usual daily life of most human beings. I like to divide denial into unconscious denial and conscious denial. *Unconscious* denial is having the past arrive and manifest in emotional or physical symptoms of addictions or illnesses without any realization that there is a connection between deep-seated needs, desires, hopes, and unfulfilled infantile needs. Past trauma or sexual abuse and present state of being can also contribute. Unconscious denial is living in this state of emotional liability, addiction, chronic physical pain, emotional pain, depression, or recurring dreams or nightmares. *Conscious* denial is listening to the symptoms of our needs, desires, hopes, dreams, and traumas and reconciling with ourselves and those who might have inflicted harm upon us. The denial is that we choose to work through some of the underlying feelings or put them on hold until another time.

An example put forth by Sigmund Freud might help explain conscious denial. One of Freud's conditions for analysis was to "act as if you are sitting at the window of a railway train and describing to someone behind you the changing views you see outside. Finally, never forget that you have promised absolute honesty, and never leave anything unsaid because for any reason it is unpleasant to say it."[1]

In conscious denial, the patient states that she understands and is aware that there is a lot of material in her utterances that needs to be interpreted. However, she chooses to relate her narrative without tracing the connections.

The thoughts said by the patient are neither being neglected nor denied. They are said, then the patient is requested to put them on hold until a later date. Together patient and listener discuss why she needs to put them aside for now. Together they make a comfortable plan for the patient, perhaps even using the techniques for changing unhealthy beliefs described in Chapter Two. The request is honored and the narrative is dealt with either in a later trimester or postpartum.

Three mothers in particular illustrate the concerns of past sexual trauma.

---

1. Sigmund Freud, *Collected Papers,* volume 2 (New York: Basic Books, Inc., 1959).

Case Study: Marisol

Marisol was brutally raped five years before her marriage. She attended a rape crisis center and seemingly let go of her past. When I met her, she was happily married and expecting her first child, due to give birth in twelve weeks. Usually upbeat with great energy, she had begun to feel fearful, however, bordering on terrified and depressed. Ostensibly, her main concern was what kind of a support person her husband would be. Her true, underlying need was this: If he is there as my support person, who will watch the door and keep the rapists out?

Marisol and her husband decided that he would play the role of her support person and her advocate with the medical staff. As her support person, he would be with her all during her labor and birth. Her brother, a man built like a linebacker, whom she trusted implicitly, would stand guard at the door of her birthing room for her entire labor and birth.

From an adaptive point of view, if Marisol had truly worked through the trauma of her rape (if anyone can ever completely do that), she would not have needed her brother guarding the doorway. Without any judgment on anyone's part, she and her entire support team accepted her need for conscious denial and dealt with it accordingly. She needed to relax and feel safe and to forget about the rape and be totally present for herself and her baby during her labor. The goal was for her to feel safe and comfortable and to have an easy vaginal birth. By acknowledging her needs and accepting herself for where she was in her process of healing from the rape, she was able to have the outcome she desired. She felt calm, centered, safe, and focused during her labor and birth.

Case Study: Lora

Lora had been raped when she was in college but had never told anyone. She hadn't received any counseling at all for her rape. In fact, she had actually repressed it, so that most of the time, if anyone brought up rape or if she read about it, she truly didn't realize that it had happened to her, too.

Lora had been married about seven years after her rape and was in her second month of pregnancy. Suffering severe anxiety and tremendous fear and guilt, Lora wanted to confide in her husband but was afraid he would leave her if he found out about the rape. She agreed that it was not too late for her to go to a rape crisis center. She was too afraid to go, however. Our goal in therapy was for her to get enough strength to attend the rape crisis center and then to have her husband in for a joint session in order for her to tell him what had happened to her. She wanted to accomplish all of this before her third trimester. She set realistic goals, and she succeeded in meeting them.

Case Study: Eileen

Eileen was three months pregnant with her first child. She was a successful professional woman, logical and organized. She had been happy, serene, and content with her life until she had a dream that her baby was going to be a boy.

She wasn't aware of her desire for either a girl or a boy for her first child. Eventually, however, she wanted to have at least one of each. Her dream was not sexual, nor were any of her associations to it. After her dream, however, she began to have tremendous anxiety, manifesting a deep-seated fear that she would molest her child. She had never been molested, to her knowledge, and she had never had a desire to molest either a boy child or a girl child. She had never molested a child.

After much deep therapy work, she was finally able to relinquish her fear, culminating in a long letter that she wrote to her uborn. The letter explained her fears and her desire to respect his mind, body, and spirit and her promise not to harm him in any way. She wrote of her oath to herself, which was that she would seek professional help if these feelings arose again and she couldn't deal with them on her own. What Eileen did was neither unconscious nor denial. Her unconscious as manifested through her dream shocked her, however. It was like a separate entity arriving from the deep, giving her an opportunity to live in fear and denial of these amazing feelings or to address them. She chose to bring them to the light and deal with them.

Eileen chose the path of courage and honesty, and consequently she didn't suffer any longer. Before she had decided to enter therapy with me to deal with her dream, she had suffered for a while and had been keeping these feelings about the dream secret. Once she dealt honestly with the feelings, she could let them go. This was a good example of the saying "You're as sick as your secrets."

NURTURING YOUR NEWBORN BABY

Once a uborn is in the world and no longer carried in her mother's body, the role of the new mother changes. It doesn't fade in importance, however. Baby's needs still are a large part of every mother's life and daily routine, even when those needs are different.

Many women have learned to fear labor and childbirth and don't really think too much about the next phase of their baby's care. They think the rest of motherhood will come naturally to them. And, of course, breastfeeding is the most natural thing a mother can do. Mother's breast milk is the ideal food for babies.

It is always fresh, it is inexpensive, and it is easier to give than formula. Breast milk provides better nutrition than formula, and it enhances the baby's immune system and prevents disease. In addition, many babies develop allergies to formula, but none are ever allergic to mother's milk. They may be uncomfortable or have an untoward reaction to something their mother ate, but all that is needed in these instances is to eliminate the food, and the baby is once again fine. Breastfeeding can prevent the baby from developing allergies later in life. Breast milk is easy to digest and helps mothers get back in shape and lose weight. It causes a hormone to be released that helps to contract the uterus and return it to normal health.

Breastfeeding also releases natural tranquilizers for both baby and mother, and it helps mother and baby bond. Nursing your baby is one of the most amazing chances for being present for another meditation. You can learn mindfulness just by watching your baby as she nurses. The most loving thing that you can do for yourself, your baby, and your partner is to truly give them your undivided presence when that is what you think you are doing.

Sometimes babies refuse mother's breast, as baby Kristina did. (See the Introduction.) This is sometimes because the baby dislikes the smell or taste of the mother's nipple. Be sure your nipples are clean. A dab of sugar on your breast can entice the baby to suckle.

During the first two weeks, baby should nurse about every one and a half to three hours, or eight to twelve times in twenty-four hours. After two weeks, she can nurse every two to three hours. Babies' bowel movements gradually increase to four or more per day, and the color changes from sticky green black on the first day to loose yellow by the end of the week. The nutritional component of breast milk changes throughout the feeding. It is necessary to alternate breasts, using the left for one feeding and the right for the next after the first few days so that the baby can receive the foremilk, low in calories but abundant in water-soluble vitamins;

the whole milk; and finally, after ten to fifteen minutes, the hind-milk, which has the highest concentration of calories. Feeding the baby only a few minutes at each breast for each feeding after the first three days can result in malnutrition. Some signs of adequate intake are ten to twelve wet diapers in twenty-four hours, steady weight gain, and contentedness after feeding.

Everything you eat will affect your baby. If either one of you has gas, boil one teaspoon of fennel seeds in one cup of water. Let this steep for about five minutes. Once it has steeped and reached a comfortable temperature, drink it. If your baby still has gas, you may give one or two drops of the fennel seed "tea" from an eyedropper. This usually helps immediately.

If your nipples are cracked, you can use ghee on them. Ghee is clarified butter that can be purchased at most supermarkets, usually in a jar. (If you have trouble finding this in your regular market, you can find it in Indian markets or other specialty food markets.) This will soften and soothe your nipples and also will not harm the baby. You can put her to breast without washing your nipple first.

Every mother should read at least one book on breastfeeding and contact the La Leche League for advice and for societal support from other mothers. (*Leche* means "milk" in Spanish.)

THE RAINBOW AND THE POT OF GOLD
FOR YOU AND YOUR BABY

Throughout the ages, women have birthed healthy babies who have grown into lovely, happy children and balanced, happy adults. These children have gone on to do the same. There is no reason for you to expect anything else for your own uborn. This is a perfectly natural expectation, but sometimes the only way to grasp this promise is to unlearn the negative expectations and beliefs we have adopted as our own. I hope that you'll see how easily you can do this and how practicing the exercises in this book can give you the happy baby and remarkable experience of birth you desire.

The experience of birth, as you've learned, isn't just about the mother and baby, however. Through the Leclaire Method, both mother and father have a safe forum in which to express and discuss their feelings. You now have a vehicle whereby you can grow and expand. As the support person, your partner helps to guide and nurture you and the uborn. Now the father also connects to his own intuitive thought, seeing when his partner needs to be touched, needs to be encouraged, needs to be calmed, or needs to be reassured and complimented.

Through the processes learned in this book, you, the mother, are able to come to terms with your baby's being a separate individual, an independent personality. Both mother and father learn that their child depends upon them for care, acceptance, and acknowledgment of his need for independence. When the mother truly realizes this separateness, she is able to birth the baby with less discomfort and more freedom and celebration. When she realizes that she is not losing a part of herself, but rather that she is giving birth to an individual, she allows herself the pleasure of an easy labor and birthing.

I wish for every mother the joy I felt with my own children and the joy I have watched grow in many mothers and fathers in my care. Each of these parents is making the world better, one baby at time, and I hope you and your baby join this new wave of peace and love. Good luck, and good wishes.

The body itself is a screen
to shield and partially reveal
the light that's blazing
inside your presence.

—RUMI

Appendix

My Meditation Goals

Week 1:

Week 2:

Week 3:

Week 4:

Week 5:

Week 6:

Week 7:

Week 8:

Week 9:

Week 10:

Week 11:

Week 12:

Week 13:

Week 14:

Week 15:

Week 16:

Week 17:

Week 18:

Week 19:

Week 20:

Week 21:

Week 22:

Week 23:

Week 24:

Week 25:

Week 26:

Week 27:

Week 28:

Week 29:

Week 30:

Week 31:

Week 32:

Week 33:

Week 34:

Week 35:

Week 36:

SAMPLE PREGNANCY HEALTH PLAN

	FIRST TRIMESTER	SECOND TRIMESTER	THIRD TRIMESTER	THREE MONTHS POSTPARTUM
Creative Thinking				
Social Support				
Nutrition				

Exercise

Play

Purpose in Life

Glossary

alpha state: The state of daydreaming and imagery; a state of peaceful relaxation characterized by alpha rhythms of the brainwaves. These rhythms can be recorded on a machine, called an electroencephalograph, that graphs brain impulses.

anchor: A circle made on the chest with the middle finger of the left hand; puts you into a deep, concentrated state of focus, or a hypnotic trance. The more you make this circle, the deeper you go into relaxation. Your anchor will work for you whenever you want it to, especially during labor, transition, and birth.

ankle pressure: A technique in which the support person squeezes the leg of the mother just above the left ankle simultaneously with her contractions. As her abdomen rises and the contraction becomes more intense and effective, so does the squeezing. Because the body is unable to experience two discomforts at the same time, the mother focuses on the hand as a support on her ankle, grounding her, sending white light into her ankle, and is not aware of the possible discomfort of the contraction.

ankle pressure for transition: This variation of the technique is particularly helpful during transition and can be used during labor to enhance opening of the cervix. It should never be practiced before the due date, however.

Ayurveda: Literally, "the science of life." This ancient healing and preventive practice has been used in India for at least five thousand years. It takes into account each individual body type and then recommends foods and health practices related to that type. The types are based on the elements: air, water, earth, and fire.

doula: An experienced woman companion in attendance to the mother at all stages of labor through birth.

left brain: The part of the brain used for analytical, linear thinking.

right brain: The part of the brain used for creative and artistic endeavors and for intuitive knowledge.

sounding: Use during labor of the vowels or of the mantras explained in Chapter Nine. Sounding refers to a controlled noise a mother makes that can facilitate birth through resonating in various parts of her body as the baby moves through the birth canal. It helps to practice these sounds, to avoid screaming, which is out-of-control sound.

support person: Usually the person who is your life partner—either the father of your child or a same-sex partner who will coparent your child. This person is also the one with whom you will attend childbirth classes and who will be present with you throughout your labor and birth.

third eye: The space between the two eyebrows; part of the system of energy centers called *chakras.* Many traditions believe the third eye is a bridge into your unconscious mind. Focusing here can be very effective.

uborn: The child who is uterine-born and uterine-borne, who is already existing and very much alive and present, but not yet visible as a being to the naked eye. The survival and birth of a healthy uborn depend upon the emotional, physical, spiritual, and nutritional well-being of the mother and on the healthy and safe environment of the family, the uterus, and the universe.

Resources

BOOKS BY MICHELLE LECLAIRE O'NEILL

Creative Childbirth: The Complete Leclaire Method (Los
  Angeles: Papyrus Press, 1993): $11.95
Leclaire Childbirth Method Workbook: $6.95
*Twelve Weeks to Fertility: The Easy Way to Conceive and
  Carry a Healthy Baby to Full Term.* (iUniverse.com,
  2000): $11.95
The Pregnancy Diary (iUniverse.com, 2000): $21.95

AUDIOTAPES AVAILABLE THROUGH MAIL ORDER

Hypnosis and Pregnancy: $9.95
Hypnosis for Labor: $9.95
Meditation and Healing: $9.95
Leclaire Smart Beginnings Music: $13.95

Package including *Creative Childbirth, Workbook,* and *Hypnosis and Pregnancy,*
Hypnosis for Labor, and *Leclaire Smart Beginnings Music* tapes: $49.95, plus $5.00 for
shipping and handling (package is sent Priority Mail)

For Mail Orders:

845 Via de la Paz, Suite 7 *or*
P.O. Box 1086
Pacific Palisades, CA 90272
Phone: 310-454-0920
or via E-mail: birthing@gte.net

Please include $5.00 for shipping (via priority mail) and handling. Thank you.

For Leclaire Method with Hypnosis Certification, which qualifies for sixteen CE credits, please call or write to the above addresses.

Suggested Reading

Gaskin, Ina May. *Spiritual Midwifery*. Summertown, Tenn.: The Book Publishing Co., 1990.

Gotsch, Gwen, and Judy Torgus. *The Womanly Art of Breastfeeding*, rev. ed. New York: Plume, 1997.

Hanh, Thich Nhat. *Breathe! You're Alive: Sutra on the Full Awareness of Breathing*. Berkeley, Calif.: Parallax Press, 1990.

Hogg, Tracy, with Linda Blau. *Secrets of the Baby Whisperer*. New York: Ballantine Books, 2001.

Lad, Usha, and Vasant Lad. *Ayurvedic Cooking for Self-Healing*. Albuquerque: Ayurvedic Press, 1997.

Liedloff, Jean. *The Continuum Concept: In Search of Happiness Lost*. New York: Warner Books, 1979.

Martin, Margaret. *The Illustrated Book of Pregnancy and Childbirth*. New York: Facts on File, 1991.

Odent, Michel. *Entering the World: The De-Medicalization of Childbirth*. New York: New American Library, 1984.

O'Neill, Michelle Leclaire. *Creative Childbirth*. Los Angeles: Papyrus Press, 1992.

———. *The Pregnancy Diary*. New York: Authors Choice Press, 2000.

———. *Twelve Weeks to Fertility*. New York: Writers Club Press, 2001.

Osmond, Marie, with Marcia Wilkie and Dr. Judita Moore. *Behind the Smile: My Journal of Postpartum Depression*. New York: Warner Books, 2001.

Samuels, Mike, and Nancy Samuels. *The New Well Pregnancy Book*. New York: Simon & Schuster, 1996.

Van der Zande, Irene. *1, 2, 3 . . . The Toddler Years*. Santa Cruz, Calif.: Santa Cruz Toddler Care Center, 1995.

Verny, Thomas, with Kelly John. *The Secret Life of the Unborn Child*. New York: Dell Publishing, 1981.

Bibliography

Chodorow, Nancy J. *The Reproduction of Mothering: Psychoanalysis and the Sociology of Gender*. Berkeley, Calif.: University of California Press, 1999.

Daly, Mary. *Gyn Ecology: The Metaethics of Radical Feminism*. Boston: Beacon Press, 1978.

Dawkins, Richard. *Climbing Mount Improbable*. New York: Norton, 1996.

De Stefano-Lewis, Kern, PHN, MSN. *Infants and Children with Prenatal Alcohol and Drug Exposure*. North Branch, Minn.: Sunrise River Press, 1995.

Gelis, Jacques, and Rosemary Morris, trans. *History of Childbirth: Fertility, Pregnancy, and Birth in Early, Modern Europe*. Boston: Northeastern University Press, 1991.

Janus, Ludwig. *The Enduring Effects of Prenatal Experience: Echoes from the Womb*. New York: Jason Aronson, 1997.

Kaplan, Louise J. *Oneness and Separateness: From Infant to Individual*. New York: Simon & Schuster, 1978.

Karr-Morse, Robin, and Meredith S. Wiley. *Ghosts from the Nursery: Tracing the Roots of Violence*. New York: Atlantic Monthly Press, 1997.

Kofman, Sarah. *The Enigma of Woman.* Ithaca, N.Y.: Cornell University Press, 1985.

Krieger, Dolores. *Accepting Your Power to Heal.* Santa Fe, N.Mex.: Bear & Co., 1993.

Kushi, Michio, and Aveline Kushi. *Macrobiotic Pregnancy and Care of the Newborn.* Tokyo: Japan Publications, 1985.

Lad, Vasant D. *Secrets of the Pulse.* Albuquerque: Ayurvedic Press, 1996.

———. *Ayurvedic Pregnancy Lectures.* Albuquerque: Ayurvedic Press, 1998.

Laughlin, Tom. *Jungian Theory and Therapy: Jungian Psychology,* Vol. 2. Los Angeles: Panarion Press, 1992.

MacLaren, Aileen, CNM, MSN. *Maternal Neonatal Nursing.* (Springhouse, Pa.: Springhouse Publishing Co, 1994.)

Nathanielsz, Peter W. *Life Before Birth: The Challenges of Fetal Development.* New York: W. H. Freeman & Co., 1992.

Niehoff, Debra. *The Biology of Violence: How Understanding the Brain, Behavior, Environment Can Break the Vicious Circle of Aggression.* New York: The Free Press, 1999.

Nilsson, Lennart. *A Child Is Born.* New York: Dell Publishing, 1986.

Perera, Sylvia Brinton. *Descent to the Goddess.* Toronto: Inner City Books, 1980.

Pert, Candace B. *Molecules of Emotion: Why You Feel the Way You Feel.* New York: Scribner, 1997.

Piontelli, Alessandra. *From Fetus to Child: An Observational and Psychoanalytical Study.* London: Routledge, 1992.

Romachandron, V. S., and Sandra Blakeslee. *Phantoms in the Brain: Probing the Mysteries of the Human Mind.* New York: William Morrow & Co., 1998.

Ruddick, Sara. *Maternal Thinking: Towards a Politics of Peace.* New York: Ballantine, 1989.

Siegal, Daniel J. *The Developing Mind.* New York: The Guilford Press, 1999.

Small, Meredith F. *Our Babies, Ourselves: How Biology and Culture Shape the Way We Parent.* New York: Doubleday, 1998.

Spong, John Shelby. *Born of a Woman: A Bishop Rethinks the Virgin Birth and the Treatment of Women by a Male-Dominated Church.* San Francisco: HarperCollins, 1992.

Vaughan, Christopher. *How Life Begins: The Science of Life in the Womb.* New York: Dell Publishing, 1996.

About the Author

Michelle Leclaire O'Neill, Ph.D., R.N., has worked in the field of psychoneuroimmunology for the past sixteen years. She was on the staff of the Simonton Cancer Center in Southern California for ten years. While there, she taught meditation; imagery; their two-year health plan, dealing with death and dying as part of life; and getting well again. As a balance to her work with cancer patients. Dr. O'Neill began working with reproductive health and preventive medicine. She developed the Leclaire Childbirth Method, the first childbirth method developed by a woman, and the Mind Body Fertility program, which she teaches at various locales. She lectures and speaks extensively on her program. She counsels and works from her Mind Body Center clinic in Pacific Palisades, California. She is the mother of three children.

Dr. O'Neill's tapes and books have made the Leclaire Method available to women who cannot attend her classes or work with her individually. The success of that program, along with recent books about the effect of the uborn's experiences in utero, prompted Dr. O'Neill to expand these concepts to nurturing both the uborn and the mother.

Dr. O'Neill is currently training other health care practitioners in the Leclaire Method. For a list of these practitioners or to consult with Dr. O'Neill about your own pregnancy, visit her Web site at http://www.leclairemethod.com; call (310) 454-0920; or send an E-mail to birthing@gte.net.

Index

acupressure, 56
acupuncture, 194
adrenaline, 51, 87
aggressive behavior, child's, 107–8
alcohol abuse, 100
Alcoholics Anonymous, 101
all-fours position, 137
alpha state, 50, 158
anchor, 68–69, 181
anemia, 220
anesthesia, 40–41, 166
Angela's Ashes, 110
ankle-squeezing technique, 56 57,
        143, 145–46, 204
Aristotle, 164
aromas and fragrances, 116–17
astringent foods, 96, 116
attachment studies, 112
Ayurvedic medicine, 4, 93, 96,
        115–16, 141

Baroque music, 152–53
beans, 94
behavioral development. *See* fetal
        development
beta state, 158
beverages, 95
Bing, Elizabeth, 166
birthing. *See* childbirth; labor
birthing chair, 165
birthing positions, traditional,
        136, 165
   all-fours, 137

   kneeling, 137
   squatting, 137
bitter foods, 96, 116
bonding, mother-infant, 5–6, 111
Bradley, Robert H., 167
brain structure, fetus, 108–10
breastfeeding, 108, 152–53, 227–29
breathing
   hypnosis and, 54–55
   meditation and, 84
breech presentation, 136

caffeine, 98, 100
Cairns, Robert, 107
calcium, 95
Care and Feeding of Children,
        The, 138
catecholemines, 51
cereals, 94
certified nurse midwife (CNM), 122
cesarean sections, 57, 166, 168
childbirth. *See also* labor; pregnancy
   conflicting attitudes about, 22–32
   early history of, 164–65, 168–69
   excitement of, 13
   myths about, 57–59, 162–64
   new ideas about, 12–13
   pain-free, 1–3
   rational beliefs about, 17–22
   traditional positions for,
        136–37, 165
   in the twentieth century, 166–69
   woman-centered approach, 3–4

247